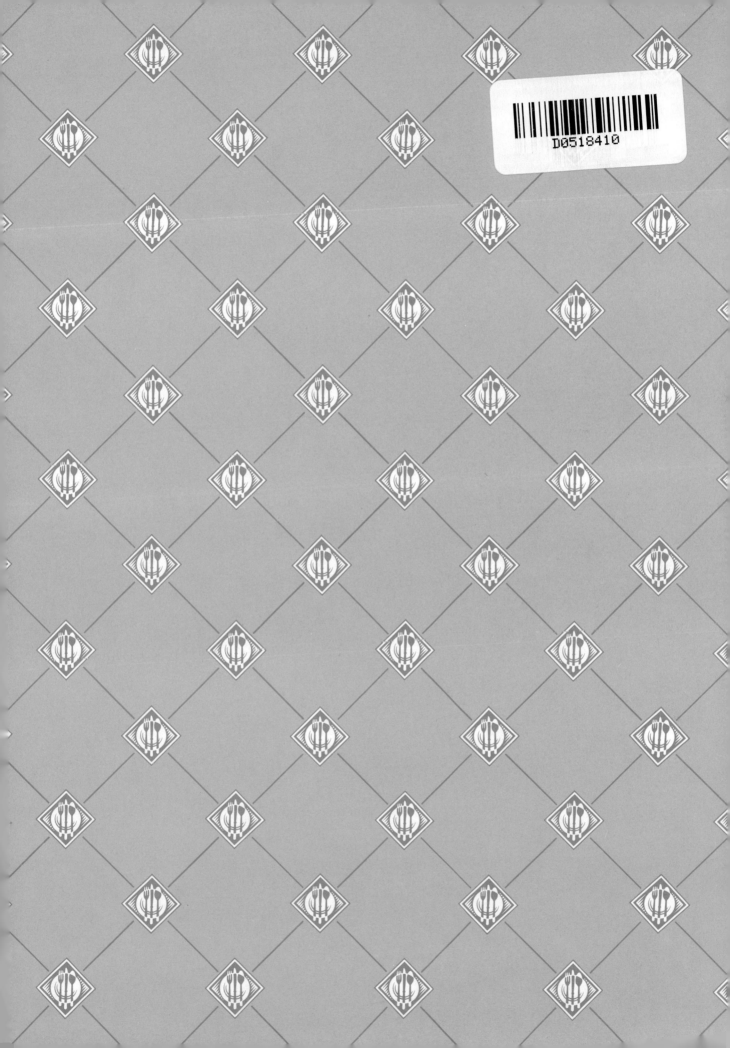

Ice Cream Delights

Frosty pies, chilly cakes,
cool drinks and more

PUBLICATIONS INTERNATIONAL, LTD.

6/97 Gift 15⁰⁰

Favorite All Time Recipes is a trademark of Publications International, Ltd.

All recipes and photographs that contain specific brand names are copyrighted by those companies and/or associations.

Some of the products listed in this publication may be in limited distribution.

Dole is a registered trademark of Dole Food Company, Inc.

Dreyer's Grand Ice Cream (available west of the Rocky Mountains) is available as Edy's Grand Ice Cream east of the Rocky Mountains.

ISBN: 1-56173-976-6

Cover photography and photography on pages 13, 16, 27, 41, 53, 71 and 81 by Sacco Productions Limited/Chicago.
Photographers: Robert Sacco, Peter Walters
Photo Stylist/Production: Betty Karslake
Food Stylists: Lois Hlavac, Gail O'Donnell, Moisette Sintov-McNerny

Photography on page 85 by Burke/Triolo Studio/Los Angeles.

Pictured on the front cover: Chocolate-Orange Dessert Sauce (*page 52*).

Pictured on the back cover (*clockwise from left*): Ice Cream Shop Pies (*page 4*), Dish of Dirt (*page 70*), and Brownie Alaska (*page 76*).

8 7 6 5 4 3 2 1

Manufactured in U.S.A.

Microwave ovens vary in wattage and power output. Cooking times given with microwave directions in this publication may need to be adjusted. Consult manufacturer's instructions for suitable microwave-safe cooking dishes.

CONTENTS

Strawberry Chocolate Roll (page 12)

CHILLY CAKES & PIES

Ice Cream Shop Pie

1½ cups cold half and half or
    milk
1 package (4-serving size)
    JELL-O® Instant Pudding
    and Pie Filling, any flavor
3½ cups COOL WHIP® Whipped
    Topping, thawed

Ice Cream Shop Ingredients
    (see page 6)
1 packaged chocolate, graham
    cracker or vanilla crumb
    crust

Pour half and half into large bowl. Add pudding mix. Beat with wire whisk until well blended, 1 to 2 minutes. Let stand 5 minutes or until slightly thickened.

Fold whipped topping and Ice Cream Shop Ingredients into pudding mixture. Spoon into crust.

Freeze pie until firm, about 6 hours or overnight. Remove from freezer. Let stand at room temperature about 10 minutes before serving to soften. Store any leftover pie in freezer.　　　　*Makes 8 servings*

Ice Cream Shop Pies (page 6): Rocky Road Pie (top); Toffee Bar Crunch Pie (center); Strawberry Banana Split Pie (bottom)

Ice Cream Shop Ingredients

Rocky Road Pie: Use any chocolate flavor pudding mix and chocolate crumb crust. Fold in ½ cup *each* BAKER'S® Semi-Sweet Real Chocolate Chips, KRAFT® Miniature Marshmallows and chopped nuts with whipped topping. Serve with chocolate sauce, if desired.

Toffee Bar Crunch Pie: Use French vanilla or vanilla flavor pudding mix and graham cracker crumb crust, spreading ⅓ cup butterscotch sauce onto bottom of crust before filling. Fold in 1 cup chopped chocolate-covered English toffee bars (about 6 bars) with whipped topping. Garnish with additional chopped toffee bars, if desired.

Strawberry Banana Split Pie: Use French vanilla or vanilla flavor pudding mix, reducing half and half to ¾ cup and adding ¾ cup puréed BIRDS EYE® Quick Thaw Strawberries with the half and half. Use vanilla crumb crust and line bottom with banana slices. Garnish with whipped topping, maraschino cherries and chopped nuts. Serve with remaining strawberries, puréed, if desired.

Chocolate Cookie Pie: Use French vanilla or vanilla flavor pudding mix and chocolate crumb crust. Fold in 1 cup chopped chocolate sandwich cookies with whipped topping.

Nutcracker Pie: Use butter pecan flavor pudding mix and graham cracker crumb crust. Fold in 1 cup chopped mixed nuts with whipped topping.

Peppermint Stick Pie: Use French vanilla or vanilla flavor pudding mix and chocolate crumb crust. Fold in ½ cup crushed hard peppermint candies, ½ cup BAKER'S® Semi-Sweet Real Chocolate Chips and 2 teaspoons peppermint extract with whipped topping.

Prep time: 15 minutes
Freezing time: 6 hours

Rainbow Sorbet Torte

Rainbow Sorbet Torte

4 pints assorted flavors sorbet
1 package DUNCAN HINES®
 White Cake Mix

Assorted fruit, for garnish

1. Line bottom of 8-inch round cake pan with aluminum foil. Soften one pint of sorbet. Spread evenly in pan. Freeze until firm. Run knife around edge of pan to loosen sorbet. Remove from pan. Wrap in foil and return to freezer. Repeat for other flavors.

2. Preheat oven to 350°F. Grease and flour two 8-inch round cake pans. Prepare, bake and cool cake following package directions for No Cholesterol recipe.

3. To assemble torte, cut both cake layers in half horizontally. Place one cake layer on serving plate. Top with one layer sorbet. Peel off foil. Repeat layers. Wrap foil around plate and cake. Return to freezer until ready to serve. To serve, garnish top with fruit.

Makes 10 to 12 servings

Tip: This is a good make-ahead dessert.

Ice Cream Party Cake

Ice Cream Party Cake

8 finger-shaped creme-filled
   chocolate snack cakes
½ gallon BORDEN® or
   MEADOW GOLD® Ice
   Cream, any flavor, slightly
   softened

1 tablespoon chocolate-flavored
   syrup
Maraschino cherries and
   whipped topping, optional
Additional chocolate-flavored
   syrup, optional

Cut 5 cakes in half crosswise, then lengthwise. In 9-inch springform
pan, place cake pieces vertically around side. Cut each remaining cake
crosswise into 8 pieces; line bottom of pan. Spoon ice cream into
prepared pan. Drizzle with chocolate syrup. Cover. Freeze overnight or
until firm. Garnish with cherries and whipped topping if desired.
Remove side of pan; let stand 10 minutes before serving. Serve with
chocolate syrup if desired. Freeze leftovers.

Makes 1 (9-inch) cake

Tip: Snack cakes slice easier when frozen or chilled.

Orange Creamsicle Pie

18 HONEY MAID® Graham
    Crackers, finely crushed
    (about 1¼ cups crumbs)
¼ cup sugar
⅓ cup BLUE BONNET®
    Margarine, melted
1 quart vanilla ice cream,
    softened

1 (6-ounce) can frozen orange
    juice concentrate, thawed
Whipped topping, for garnish
Orange slices, for garnish

In small bowl, combine crumbs, sugar and margarine; press onto bottom and side of 9-inch pie plate. Set aside.

In large bowl, with electric mixer on medium speed, blend ice cream and orange juice concentrate; spread in prepared crust. Freeze until firm, about 4 hours. Before serving, garnish with whipped topping and orange slices, if desired.
Makes 8 servings

Pineapple Mincemeat Ice Cream Pie

1½ cups gingersnap cookie
    crumbs
¼ cup margarine, melted
1 can (20 ounces) DOLE®
    Crushed Pineapple in juice,
    drained
2 cups mincemeat
2 tablespoons brandy, optional
1 quart vanilla ice cream,
    softened

1 cup whipping cream, whipped
1 can (8 ounces) DOLE®
    Crushed Pineapple in juice,
    drained
2 tablespoons DOLE® Slivered
    Almonds, toasted (see Tip
    page 39)

Combine gingersnap crumbs and margarine in small bowl. Press into 8- or 9-inch springform pan.

Combine 20-ounce can pineapple, mincemeat and brandy with softened ice cream in large bowl. Pour into springform pan. Freeze until firm.

Remove from freezer 15 minutes before serving. Garnish with whipped cream, 8-ounce can pineapple and almonds.
Makes 10 servings

Angel Food Surprise Cake

1 purchased round angel food
    cake (about 19 ounces)
1 quart strawberry ice cream,
    softened
1 pint lime sherbet, softened
1½ cups whipping cream

3 tablespoons confectioners'
    sugar
½ teaspoon vanilla extract
    Whole fresh strawberries,
    optional
    Lime slices, optional

Place cake on foil-covered cardboard square. To make cake shell, cut down into cake with serrated knife, ½-inch from inner and outer edges. Carefully remove cake (reserve for another use), forming a hollow center; leave 1-inch-thick base. Freeze cake about 1 hour.

Carefully fill hollow portion with strawberry ice cream, being sure to pack ice cream firmly to avoid any air spaces from forming. Return to freezer until firm, about 3 hours. Fill center portion of cake with lime sherbet. Cover; freeze several hours or overnight.

About 1 hour before serving, place cake on serving plate. Combine whipping cream, sugar and vanilla in small chilled mixing bowl. Whip until stiff peaks form. Frost sides and top of cake. Return to freezer until ready to serve. For ease in slicing, remove cake and let stand at room temperature about 15 minutes before serving. Garnish with strawberries and lime slices, if desired. *Makes 10 to 12 servings*

Favorite recipe from **American Dairy Association**

Frozen Peach Melba Pie

2 cups crushed *granola or*
    natural cereal
3 tablespoons *flour*
3 tablespoons *margarine or*
    butter, melted
2 teaspoons *ground cinnamon*
1 (10-ounce) package *frozen*
    red raspberries in syrup,
    thawed and drained,
    reserving ⅔ cup syrup

¼ cup *red currant jelly or red*
    raspberry jam
1 tablespoon *cornstarch*
¼ teaspoon *almond extract*
½ (½ gallon) carton *BORDEN®*
    or MEADOW GOLD®
    Peach Premium Frozen
    Yogurt

Preheat oven to 375°F. In medium bowl, combine granola, flour, margarine and cinnamon; press onto bottom and up side to rim of 9-inch pie plate to form crust. Bake 8 to 10 minutes. Cool.

In small saucepan, combine reserved raspberry syrup, jelly and cornstarch. Over medium heat, cook and stir until slightly thickened and glossy; stir in extract and raspberries. Cool. Scoop frozen yogurt into prepared crust; top with raspberry sauce. Freeze 6 hours or until firm. Remove from freezer 5 to 10 minutes before serving. Garnish as desired. Freeze ungarnished leftovers. *Makes 1 (9-inch) pie*

Ice Cream Cakes

2¾ cups sifted cake flour
1⅔ cups sugar
4½ teaspoons baking powder
  1 teaspoon salt
1⅓ cups milk, divided
  ⅔ cup CRISCO® Shortening
  5 egg whites
  1 teaspoon vanilla extract

½ gallon chocolate ice cream, softened
2 jars (8 ounces each) maraschino cherries, drained and cut into halves
1 cup chopped walnuts
6 cups whipped topping

1. Preheat oven to 350°F.

2. For cake, combine cake flour, sugar, baking powder and salt in a large mixer bowl. Add 1 cup milk and Crisco. Blend at low speed of electric mixer. Beat for 2 minutes at medium speed (or beat vigorously by hand about 300 strokes). Add egg whites, remaining ⅓ cup milk and vanilla. Continue beating for 2 minutes.

3. Pour batter into 2 greased and floured 9-inch round pans.

4. Bake at 350°F for 25 to 30 minutes or until toothpick inserted in center comes out clean.

5. Cool for 10 minutes in pans on racks, remove from pans. Cool on racks.

6. Mix ice cream, cherries and nuts. Divide evenly in 2 foil-lined 9-inch round pans. Freeze until firm.

7. For each cake, place 1 cooled cake layer on foil-covered cardboard round. Remove 1 ice cream layer from pan; peel off foil and place ice cream on cake. Frost sides and top of each cake with half of whipped topping.

8. Freeze until firm. Let soften slightly before serving.

Makes 2 (9-inch) cakes

Strawberry Chocolate Roll

3 large eggs, separated
½ cup sugar
5 ounces semisweet chocolate,
    melted
⅓ cup water
1 teaspoon vanilla
¾ cup all-purpose flour
1 teaspoon baking powder

½ teaspoon baking soda
¼ teaspoon salt
    Unsweetened cocoa
½ cup seedless strawberry or
    raspberry jam
2 pints strawberry ice cream,
    softened

Preheat oven to 350°F. Line 15×10-inch jelly-roll pan with foil, extending foil 1 inch over ends of pan. Grease and flour foil.

Beat egg yolks and sugar in medium bowl until light and fluffy. Beat in melted chocolate. Add water and vanilla. Mix until smooth. Sift flour, baking powder, baking soda and salt together. Add to chocolate mixture.

Using clean beaters and large bowl, beat egg whites until soft peaks form. Gently fold in chocolate mixture. Pour into prepared pan.

Bake 8 to 9 minutes or until wooden pick inserted into center comes out clean. Carefully loosen sides of cake from foil. Invert cake onto towel sprinkled with cocoa. Peel off foil. Starting at short end, roll warm cake, jelly-roll fashion with towel inside. Cool cake completely.

Unroll cake and remove towel. Spread cake with jam. Spread ice cream, leaving a ¼-inch border. Roll up cake. Wrap tightly in plastic wrap or foil. Freeze. Allow cake to stand at room temperature 10 minutes before cutting and serving.   *Makes 8 to 12 servings*

Strawberry Chocolate Roll

Strawberry Pie

CRUST

3½ cups Rice CHEX® brand
    cereal, crushed to 1 cup
¼ cup packed brown sugar

⅓ cup flaked coconut
⅓ cup margarine or butter,
    melted

FILLING

1 pint strawberries, hulled
3 tablespoons granulated sugar

1 quart vanilla ice cream,
    softened

To prepare crust, preheat oven to 300°F. Grease 9-inch pie plate. Combine cereal, brown sugar and coconut. Add margarine. Mix thoroughly. Press evenly onto bottom and up side of prepared pie plate. Bake 10 minutes. Cool completely.

To prepare filling, reserve 5 berries for garnish. Mash remaining berries. Combine with granulated sugar. Mix into ice cream until thoroughly blended. Turn into crust. Freeze 4 to 5 hours or until firm. To serve, garnish with reserved berries. *Makes 6 to 8 servings*

Black Magic Pie

42 OREO® Chocolate Sandwich
    Cookies
2 tablespoons BLUE BONNET®
    Margarine, melted
1 quart chocolate ice cream

1 pint vanilla ice cream,
    softened
½ cup whipped topping
    Chocolate fudge sauce

Finely crush 22 cookies. Mix 1¼ cups cookie crumbs and margarine; set aside remaining crumbs. Press onto bottom of 9-inch pie plate. Stand 14 cookies around edge of plate, pressing lightly into crust.

Scoop chocolate ice cream into balls; arrange in prepared crust. Coarsely chop remaining 6 cookies; sprinkle over ice cream scoops. Spread softened vanilla ice cream evenly over cookie layer; freeze 15 minutes. Top with a layer of reserved cookie crumbs, pressing gently into ice cream. Freeze several hours or overnight. To serve, garnish with whipped topping and fudge sauce. *Makes 8 servings*

Banana Split Pie

Banana Split Pie

20 chocolate sandwich cookies
¼ cup margarine, melted
2 medium DOLE® Bananas,
   peeled, sliced
1 quart strawberry ice cream,
   softened

1 can (20 ounces) DOLE®
   Crushed Pineapple in juice,
   drained
1 cup whipping cream, whipped
¼ cup chopped nuts
   Maraschino cherry, optional

For crust, pulverize cookies in food processor or blender. Add melted margarine. Process until blended. Press into 9-inch pie plate. Bake in 350°F oven 5 minutes. Cool.

Arrange sliced bananas over crust. Spread ice cream over bananas. Add pineapple. Cover pie with whipped cream. Sprinkle with nuts. Freeze 4 hours or until firm. Remove from freezer 30 minutes before cutting. Garnish with maraschino cherry, if desired. *Makes 8 servings*

Prep time: 20 minutes
Baking time: 5 minutes
Freezing time: 4 hours

Frozen Chocolate Cheesecake

Frozen Chocolate Cheesecake

1½ cups chocolate or vanilla
    wafer cookie crumbs
⅓ cup margarine, melted
1 package (8 ounces) cream
    cheese, softened
½ cup sugar, divided
2 eggs,* separated

1 cup semisweet chocolate
    chips, melted
1 teaspoon vanilla
1 cup whipping cream, lightly
    whipped
¾ cup chopped pecans
    Chocolate Curls, recipe
    follows

Preheat oven to 325°F. Combine crumbs and margarine; press on bottom and up side of 9-inch pie plate. Bake 10 minutes. Cool completely on wire rack.

Combine cream cheese and ¼ cup sugar in large bowl. Beat egg yolks; gradually stir into cheese mixture with melted chocolate chips and vanilla. Beat egg whites in small bowl until foamy. Gradually add remaining ¼ cup sugar, beating until soft peaks form. Gently fold egg whites into chocolate mixture. Fold in whipped cream and pecans. Pour chocolate filling into prepared crust and freeze until firm. Garnish with chocolate curls.

Makes about 8 servings

*Use only grade A clean, uncracked eggs.

Chocolate Curls

Melt ¾ cup semisweet chocolate chips in small saucepan over low heat. Spread layer on cold baking sheet. Refrigerate until firm, 15 minutes. Slip tip of straight-sided metal spatula under chocolate. Push spatula firmly along baking sheet, so chocolate curls as it is pushed up. Place curls on waxed paper.

Piña Colada Pie

1 can (20 ounces) DOLE®
    Crushed Pineapple in juice,
    drained
3 tablespoons dark rum
3 tablespoons canned cream of
    coconut

1 quart vanilla ice cream,
    softened
Flaked coconut, optional
DOLE® Pineapple, optional

COCONUT CRUST
1½ cups vanilla wafer crumbs
   1 cup flaked coconut, toasted
   (see Tip below)

¼ cup margarine, melted

Stir pineapple, rum and cream of coconut into ice cream in large bowl. Freeze until ice cream holds shape.

Combine all crust ingredients. Press onto bottom and up side of 9-inch pie plate. Place in freezer until firm. Spoon filling into crust. Cover with plastic wrap and freeze overnight or until firm enough to cut. Garnish with additional coconut and pineapple, if desired.

Makes 8 servings

Prep time: 15 minutes
Freezing time: 4 hours

Tip: To toast coconut, spread coconut on baking sheet. Bake at 350°F 7 to 15 minutes or until golden, stirring frequently; cool.

Green Mountain Pie in Chewy Crust

CRUST
1¾ cups soft macaroon crumbs
   (about seven 2-inch
   macaroons crumbled with
   fingers)

¼ cup BUTTER FLAVOR
   CRISCO®, melted

FILLING
2 pints lime sherbet, softened
1 quart vanilla ice cream,
   softened

1½ cups soft macaroon crumbs

1. **For crust**, preheat oven to 350°F. Lightly grease 9-inch pie plate.

2. Combine 1¾ cups crumbs and melted Butter Flavor Crisco. Press into greased pie plate.

3. Bake at 350°F for 10 minutes. Cool completely before filling.

4. **For filling**, spread 1 pint sherbet in cooled crust. Freeze about 1 hour or until firm.

5. Combine ice cream and 1½ cups crumbs. Spread evenly over sherbet. Freeze about 1 hour or until firm.

6. Spread remaining sherbet over ice cream. Freeze several hours. Remove from freezer 10 to 15 minutes before slicing.

Makes 1 (9-inch) pie or 8 servings

Note: Lemon sherbet may be used in place of lime.

Chocolate & Vanilla Cake Roll

½ cup unsifted flour	*2 tablespoons water*
3 tablespoons unsweetened cocoa	*½ teaspoon vanilla extract*
1 teaspoon baking powder	*Vegetable cooking spray*
⅛ teaspoon salt	*½ (½-gallon) container*
3 eggs, separated	*BORDEN® or MEADOW*
1 egg white	*GOLD® Vanilla Premium*
¼ cup plus 3 tablespoons sugar	*Frozen Yogurt, softened*

Preheat oven to 375°F. Line 15×10-inch baking pan with aluminum foil, extending foil 1 inch over ends of pan. In small bowl, combine flour, cocoa, baking powder and salt. In another small bowl, beat *egg yolks* until thick and lemon-colored; gradually beat in *¼ cup* sugar. Add water and vanilla; mix well. In large mixer bowl, beat *4 egg whites* to soft peaks; gradually add *remaining 3 tablespoons* sugar, beating until stiff. Fold egg yolk mixture into egg whites; gently stir in flour mixture.

Pour batter into prepared pan. Bake 10 to 12 minutes or until wooden pick inserted near center comes out clean. *Immediately* turn out onto large sheet of wax paper sprayed with vegetable cooking spray. Peel off foil. Beginning at narrow end, roll up cake, jelly-roll fashion. Cool. Unroll; spread with frozen yogurt. Roll up; cover and freeze. Garnish as desired. Freeze leftovers. *Makes 10 servings*

Kahlúa® Ice Cream Pie

1 (9-ounce) package chocolate
   wafer cookies
½ cup unsalted butter, melted
10 tablespoons KAHLÚA®,
   divided
1 teaspoon espresso powder
3 ounces semi-sweet chocolate,
   chopped

1 tablespoon unsalted butter
1 pint vanilla, coffee or
   chocolate chip ice cream
1 pint chocolate ice cream
¾ cup whipping cream, whipped
Chocolate-covered coffee
   beans, for garnish

In food processor, place about half of cookies, breaking into pieces.
Process to make fine crumbs. Repeat with remaining cookies. Add ½
cup melted butter and process with on-off pulses, just to blend. Press
crumbs evenly onto bottom and up side of 9-inch pie plate. Press
crumbs evenly to rim. Bake at 325°F for 10 minutes. Cool completely.

In small saucepan, heat 6 tablespoons Kahlúa and espresso powder over
low heat until warmed and espresso powder has dissolved. Stir in
chocolate and 1 tablespoon butter and stir until melted and smooth.
Cool completely.

Transfer vanilla ice cream to electric mixer bowl and allow to soften
slightly. Add 2 tablespoons Kahlúa and beat on low speed to blend.
Spread over bottom of cooled crust and freeze until firm. Spread cooled
chocolate mixture over ice cream in pie. Freeze until firm.

Transfer chocolate ice cream to mixer bowl and blend in remaining 2
tablespoons Kahlúa as above. Spread chocolate ice cream over sauce in
pie. Freeze until firm.

To serve, pipe decorative border of whipped cream on pie around inside
edge. Garnish with chocolate-covered coffee beans.

Makes 1 (9-inch) pie

Hot Fudge Sundae Cake

Hot Fudge Sundae Cake

1 package DUNCAN HINES®
    Moist Deluxe Dark Dutch
    Fudge Cake Mix

½ gallon brick vanilla ice cream

FUDGE SAUCE
1 can (12 ounces) evaporated
    milk
1¼ cups sugar
4 squares (1 ounce each)
    unsweetened chocolate

¼ cup butter or margarine
1½ teaspoons vanilla extract
¼ teaspoon salt
    Whipped cream, maraschino
    cherries, for garnish

1. Preheat oven to 350°F. Grease and flour 13×9×2-inch pan. Prepare, bake and cool cake following package directions.

2. Remove cake from pan. Split cake in half horizontally. Place bottom layer back in pan. Cut ice cream into even slices and place evenly over bottom cake layer (use all the ice cream). Place remaining cake layer over ice cream. Cover and freeze.

3. **For fudge sauce**, combine evaporated milk and sugar in medium saucepan. Stir constantly on medium heat until mixture comes to a rolling boil. Boil and stir for 1 minute. Add unsweetened chocolate and stir until melted. Beat over medium heat until smooth. Remove from heat. Stir in butter, vanilla and salt.

4. Cut cake into serving squares. For each serving, place cake square on plate, spoon hot fudge sauce on top. Garnish with whipped cream and maraschino cherry. *Makes 12 to 16 servings*

Tip: Fudge sauce may be prepared ahead and refrigerated in tightly sealed jar. Reheat when ready to serve.

Patriotic Pie

Patriotic Pie

CRUST
1 package DUNCAN HINES®
Blueberry Muffin Mix,
separated

¼ cup butter or margarine

FILLING
1 quart vanilla ice cream,
softened (see Tip below)

½ cup crumb mixture, reserved
from crust

TOPPING
Can of blueberries from Mix
1 pint fresh strawberries,
rinsed, drained and sliced

2 tablespoons sugar (optional)

1. Preheat oven to 400°F. Grease 9-inch pie plate.

2. **For crust**, place muffin mix and butter in medium bowl. Cut in butter with pastry blender or 2 knives until mixture is crumbly. Spread evenly in ungreased 9-inch square baking pan. *Do not press.* Bake at 400°F for 10 to 12 minutes. Stir. Cool slightly. Reserve ½ cup crumbs for filling. Press remaining crumbs onto bottom and up side of prepared pie plate to form crust. Cool completely.

3. **For filling**, spread softened ice cream over crust. Sprinkle with reserved crumbs. Freeze several hours or until firm.

4. **For topping**, rinse blueberries with cold water and drain. Combine strawberries and sugar, if desired.

5. To serve, let pie stand 5 minutes at room temperature. Cut into 8 wedges using sharp knife. Top with blueberries and strawberries.

Makes 8 servings

Tip: Ice cream can be softened by allowing to stand at room temperature for 15 minutes or placing in refrigerator for 30 minutes.

Double Chocolate Alaska Pie

CRUST
1/3 cup margarine or butter, melted

1/4 cup packed brown sugar

1 tablespoon cocoa

4 cups Rice CHEX® brand cereal, crushed to 1 cup

FILLING-MERINGUE
1 quart chocolate ice cream, softened

3 egg whites

1/2 teaspoon vanilla extract

1/4 teaspoon cream of tartar

6 tablespoons granulated sugar

To prepare crust, preheat oven to 300°F. Grease 9-inch pie plate. Combine margarine, sugar and cocoa in large bowl. Add cereal; mix thoroughly. Press evenly onto bottom and up side of prepared pie plate. Bake 10 minutes. Cool completely.

To prepare filling, fill crust with ice cream. Freeze until firm, 6 hours or overnight.

To prepare meringue, beat egg whites with vanilla and cream of tartar in medium bowl until soft peaks form. Gradually add sugar. Beat until stiff and glossy and all sugar is dissolved. Spread meringue over ice cream. Seal to edges* and freeze. At serving time bake in preheated 475°F oven about 2½ minutes or until very lightly browned. Watch closely. Serve immediately.

Makes 6 to 8 servings

*May be baked at this point according to above directions and frozen. Let stand a few minutes before serving.

Note: Best if held in freezer no longer than 2 days.

Rainbow Ice Cream Cake

2 cups coconut bar cookie crumbs

4 ounces semisweet chocolate, finely chopped

1/3 cup chopped pecans

1/3 cup butter, melted

1 quart pistachio or mint chocolate chip ice cream, softened

1 quart vanilla ice cream, softened

1 quart strawberry ice cream, softened

Sweetened whipped cream, optional

Fresh whole strawberries, optional

Combine crumbs, chocolate, nuts and butter in medium bowl; mix well. Press one third of mixture onto bottom of 9-inch springform pan. Freeze until firm. Spread pistachio ice cream over crumb mixture. Press another third of crumb mixture into top of ice cream. Return to freezer until firm. Repeat with vanilla ice cream and crumbs. Top with strawberry ice cream. Cover and freeze entire cake several hours or overnight.

To serve cake, place springform pan on serving plate. Run spatula around edge of pan. Carefully remove side. Using pastry bag, pipe whipped cream around edge of cake. Cake may be returned to freezer up to 1 hour before serving. Just before serving, decorate top of cake with fresh whole strawberries, if desired.   *Makes 1 (9-inch) cake*

Favorite recipe from **American Dairy Association**

Mississippi Mud Pie

1½ cups confectioners' sugar
½ cup whipping cream
6 tablespoons (¾ stick) butter
3 envelopes (3 oz.) NESTLÉ®
    Choco Bake pre-melted
    unsweetened baking
    chocolate flavor
3 tablespoons light corn syrup

Dash salt
1 teaspoon vanilla extract
1 9-inch prepared chocolate
    crumb crust
¾ cup chopped pecans, divided
    About 3 pints coffee ice cream
    Whipped cream for garnish

In small saucepan, combine confectioners' sugar, cream, butter, Nestlé Choco Bake unsweetened baking chocolate flavor, corn syrup and salt. Cook over low heat, stirring constantly, until mixture is smooth. Stir in vanilla. Cool to room temperature.

Spread about ½ cup of chocolate mixture in bottom of pie crust; sprinkle with ¼ cup chopped pecans. Using flat ice cream spade or large spoon, scoop thin slices of ice cream, layering about half of ice cream in pie crust. Repeat chocolate mixture and pecan layers once; top with remaining ice cream. Freeze at least 4 hours or until firm.

Drizzle remaining chocolate mixture over top of pie; sprinkle with remaining ¼ cup pecans. Garnish with whipped cream, if desired.

Makes 8 servings

Rainbow Party Punch (page 31)

FROSTY DRINKS

Sunshine Float

½ cup LIPTON® Lemon
    Flavored Ice Tea Mix
    Sweetened with
    NutraSweet®

1 quart water
1 can (6 ounces) frozen orange
    juice concentrate, thawed
Vanilla ice cream

In large pitcher, combine all ingredients except ice cream. To serve, place 1 scoop ice cream into tall glass; fill with ice tea mixture.

Makes about 5 servings

Strawberry Soda

½ cup sliced fresh strawberries
1 pint strawberry ice cream,
    softened

1½ cups chilled creme soda
Whipped cream
Fresh whole strawberries

Mash strawberries until almost smooth. Stir together half the ice cream and one third of the creme soda. Layer ice cream mixture, then strawberries in 3 tall chilled glasses. Place 1 scoop ice cream in each glass. Pour in enough soda to cover. Garnish each with whipped cream and a fresh whole strawberry. *Makes 3 servings*

Favorite recipe from **American Dairy Association**

Sunshine Float

Top to bottom: Choco-Berry Cooler;
Chocolate Root Beer Float (page 30); Frozen Banana Smoothie

Frozen Banana Smoothie

1 cup cold milk or half-and-half
½ cup mashed ripe banana
   (about 1 medium)
½ cup creme de banana liqueur

⅓ cup HERSHEY'S® Syrup
2½ cups ice cubes
Mint leaves, optional

In blender container, place all ingredients. Cover; blend on high speed 2 minutes. Decrease speed; blend 1 minute longer or until frothy. Garnish with mint leaves, if desired. Serve immediately.

Makes about 3 (9-ounce) servings

Choco-Berry Cooler

¾ cup cold milk
¼ cup sliced fresh strawberries
2 tablespoons HERSHEY'S®
   Syrup
2 tablespoons plus 2 small
   scoops vanilla ice cream,
   divided

Chilled ginger ale or club soda
Fresh strawberry, optional
Mint leaves, optional

In blender container, place milk, strawberries, syrup and 2 tablespoons vanilla ice cream; cover and blend on high speed until smooth. In ice cream soda glass, alternate remaining 2 scoops ice cream and chocolate-fruit mixture; fill glass with ginger ale. Garnish with fresh strawberry and mint leaves, if desired. Serve immediately.

Makes 1 (14-ounce) serving

Variations

Before blending, substitute one of the following fruits for fresh strawberries:

• 3 tablespoons frozen strawberries with syrup, thawed
• ½ of peeled fresh peach or ⅓ cup canned peach slices
• 2 slices canned pineapple or ¼ cup canned crushed pineapple
• ¼ cup sweetened fresh raspberries or 3 tablespoons frozen raspberries with syrup, thawed

Chocolate Root Beer Float

1 tablespoon sugar
2 teaspoons HERSHEY'S®
  Cocoa

1 tablespoon hot water
1 scoop vanilla ice cream
Chilled root beer

In 12-ounce glass, stir together sugar and cocoa; stir in water. Add ice cream; fill glass with root beer. Stir; serve immediately.

Makes 1 (12-ounce) serving

Party Punch

SHERBET RING
  1 pint lemon sherbet

1 pint lime sherbet

PUNCH
  1 can (1 quart 14 ounces)
    orange-grapefruit juice,
    chilled
  1 can (1 quart 14 ounces)
    pineapple juice, chilled

1 can (12 ounces) apricot
    nectar, chilled
¼ cup sugar
1 quart ginger ale, chilled

For sherbet ring, alternate scoops of lemon and lime sherbet in 4½-cup ring mold; pack tightly. Freeze until firm.

For punch, combine orange-grapefruit juice, pineapple juice, apricot nectar and sugar in punch bowl. Add ginger ale. To unmold sherbet ring, dip mold in warm water just to the rim for a few seconds. Invert onto flat plate and slide into punch bowl. Serve immediately.

Makes 1 gallon or 8 to 10 servings

Favorite recipe from **American Dairy Association**

Frosty Mocha

½ cup boiling water
⅓ cup NESTLÉ® Toll House®
    semi-sweet chocolate
    morsels

1 to 2 teaspoons TASTER'S
    CHOICE® Instant Coffee
1 cup ice (about 7 cubes)
1 cup vanilla ice cream

In blender container, combine boiling water, Nestlé Toll House semi-sweet chocolate morsels and instant coffee. Cover; blend on high speed until chocolate is melted. Add ice. Cover; blend 1 minute. Add ice cream. Cover; blend until smooth. Serve immediately.

Makes 2 (1-cup) servings

Rainbow Party Punch

Rainbow Party Punch

1 (4-serving size) package
   lemon, lime, orange,
   raspberry or strawberry
   flavor gelatin
1½ cups sugar
2 cups boiling water
1 (46-ounce) can pineapple
   juice, chilled

2 cups REALEMON® Lemon
   Juice from Concentrate
1 quart BORDEN® or
   MEADOW GOLD® sherbet,
   any flavor
1 (32-ounce) bottle club soda,
   chilled

In medium bowl, dissolve gelatin and sugar in boiling water; set aside.
In large punch bowl, combine pineapple juice, ReaLemon brand and
gelatin mixture. Chill. Just before serving, add sherbet and club soda.

Makes about 3½ quarts

Banana Date Milk Shake

1 frozen ripe DOLE® Banana*
½ cup milk

½ cup vanilla ice cream
¼ cup DOLE® Chopped Dates

Slice banana into blender. Add remaining ingredients. Blend on high
speed until smooth.   *Makes 1 to 2 servings*

*Peel, then freeze banana overnight in airtight plastic bag.

Clockwise from top: Fruit Flavor Milk Shake; Frosty Pudding Milk Shake; Easy Pudding Milk Shake

Frosty Pudding Milk Shakes

2 cups cold milk
1 package (4-serving size)
JELL-O® Instant Pudding
and Pie Filling, any flavor

1 pint ice cream, any flavor
Club soda

Pour milk into blender container. Add pudding mix and ice cream; cover. Blend at high speed 30 seconds. Scrape sides of container; blend 30 seconds longer. Pour into glasses. Top with club soda. Serve immediately.   *Makes about 5 cups or 4 to 6 servings*

Prep time: 5 minutes

Easy Pudding Milk Shakes

3 cups cold milk
1 package (4-serving size)
JELL-O® Instant Pudding
and Pie Filling, any flavor

1½ cups ice cream, any flavor

Pour milk into blender container. Add pudding mix and ice cream; cover. Blend at high speed 30 seconds or until smooth. Pour into glasses. Serve immediately. (Mixture thickens as it stands. Thin with additional milk, if desired.)   *Makes about 5 cups or 4 to 6 servings*

Prep time: 5 minutes

Fruit Flavor Milk Shakes

2 cups cold milk
1 package (4-serving size)
   JELL-O® Brand Gelatin, any
   flavor

1 pint vanilla ice cream

Pour milk into blender container. Add gelatin and ice cream; cover. Blend at high speed 30 seconds or until smooth. Pour into glasses. Serve immediately. *Makes about 4 cups or 4 servings*

Prep time: 5 minutes

Lime Tea Refresher

1 can (6 ounces) frozen limeade
   concentrate, thawed slightly
1/3 cup unsweetened instant tea
3 tablespoons honey

2 cups cold milk
1 pint vanilla ice cream,
   softened
Lime slices, optional

Place limeade concentrate, tea, honey and milk in blender container; cover. Blend until well combined. Add ice cream. Blend on high speed until smooth and frothy. Serve immediately in tall chilled glasses. Garnish each with lime slice. *Makes about 5 cups*

Favorite recipe from **American Dairy Association**

Raspberry Champagne Punch

2 (10-ounce) packages frozen
   red raspberries in syrup,
   thawed
1/2 cup sugar
1/3 cup REALEMON® Lemon
   Juice from Concentrate
1 (750 mL) bottle red rosé
   wine, chilled

1 quart BORDEN® or
   MEADOW GOLD®
   Raspberry Sherbet
1 (750 mL) bottle champagne,
   chilled

In blender container, purée raspberries. In large punch bowl, combine puréed raspberries, sugar, ReaLemon brand and wine; stir until sugar dissolves. Just before serving, scoop sherbet into punch bowl; add champagne. Stir gently. *Makes about 3 quarts*

Fruit Flavor Freeze (page 43)

HOMEMADE ICE CREAM

Double Almond Ice Cream

3 cups whipping cream	1 tablespoon vanilla extract
1 cup milk	2 teaspoons almond extract
¾ cup plus 2 tablespoons sugar, divided	2 tablespoons butter
4 egg yolks, beaten	1½ cups BLUE DIAMOND® Chopped Natural Almonds

Combine cream, milk and ¾ cup sugar in medium saucepan. Cook and stir over medium heat until sugar is dissolved and mixture is hot. Gradually add 1 cup cream mixture to beaten egg yolks, whisking constantly. When mixture is smooth, strain into double boiler. Gradually pour in remaining cream mixture, whisking constantly. Cook over simmering water, stirring until mixture thickens slightly and coats the back of a spoon, about 8 minutes. *Do not boil.* Stir in extracts. Cool.

Meanwhile, melt butter and stir in remaining 2 tablespoons sugar in small saucepan. Cook and stir over medium heat until sugar begins to bubble (about 30 seconds). Add almonds and cook and stir over medium heat until golden and well coated; cool. Stir almonds into cream mixture. Pour into ice cream freezer container. Freeze according to manufacturer's instructions. *Makes 1 quart*

Double Almond Ice Cream

Coffee Brickle Ice Cream

2 tablespoons instant coffee
2 teaspoons hot water
1 (14-ounce) can EAGLE®
   Brand Sweetened
   Condensed Milk (NOT
   evaporated milk)
4 cups (1 quart) BORDEN® or
   MEADOW GOLD®
   Half-and-Half

¾ cup chopped almonds, toasted
   (see Tip page 39)
⅓ cup almond brickle chips
2 teaspoons vanilla extract
1 teaspoon almond extract

In small bowl, dissolve coffee in water. In ice cream freezer container, combine all ingredients; mix well. Freeze according to manufacturer's instructions. Freeze leftovers.   *Makes about 2 quarts*

Fudgy Rocky Road Ice Cream

5 (1-ounce) squares
   unsweetened chocolate,
   melted
1 (14-ounce) can EAGLE®
   Brand Sweetened
   Condensed Milk (NOT
   evaporated milk)
2 teaspoons vanilla extract
2 cups (1 pint) BORDEN® or
   MEADOW GOLD®
   Half-and-Half

2 cups (1 pint) BORDEN® or
   MEADOW GOLD®
   Whipping Cream,
   unwhipped
1½ cups CAMPFIRE® Miniature
   Marshmallows
¾ cup chopped peanuts

In large mixer bowl, beat chocolate, sweetened condensed milk and vanilla. Stir in remaining ingredients. Pour into ice cream freezer container. Freeze according to manufacturer's instructions. Freeze leftovers.   *Makes about 2 quarts*

Fudgy Chocolate Chip Ice Cream: Omit marshmallows and reduce peanuts to ½ cup. Add ¾ cup mini chocolate chips. Proceed as above.

Left to right: Fudgy Rocky Road Ice Cream; Cherry Cheesecake Ice Cream

Cherry Cheesecake Ice Cream

1 (3-ounce) package cream cheese, softened
1 (14-ounce) can EAGLE® Brand Sweetened Condensed Milk (NOT evaporated milk)
2 cups (1 pint) BORDEN® or MEADOW GOLD® Half-and-Half

2 cups (1 pint) BORDEN® or MEADOW GOLD® Whipping Cream, unwhipped
1 (10-ounce) jar maraschino cherries, well drained and chopped (about 1 cup)
1 tablespoon vanilla extract
½ teaspoon almond extract

In large mixer bowl, beat cream cheese until fluffy. Gradually beat in sweetened condensed milk until smooth. Add remaining ingredients; mix well. Pour into ice cream freezer container. Freeze according to manufacturer's instructions. Freeze leftovers.

Makes about 1½ quarts

Tip: 1 (17-ounce) can pitted dark sweet cherries, well drained and chopped, can be substituted for maraschino cherries.

Frozen Passion

2 (14-ounce) cans EAGLE®
  Brand Sweetened
  Condensed Milk (NOT
  evaporated milk)

1 (2-liter) bottle or
  5 (12-ounce) cans
  carbonated beverage, any
  flavor
Chocolate Ice Cream Cups

In ice cream freezer container, combine all ingredients except Chocolate Ice Cream Cups; mix well. Freeze according to manufacturer's instructions. Scoop into Chocolate Ice Cream Cups. Freeze leftovers.

Makes 2 to 3 quarts

Chocolate Ice Cream Cups

2 cups (12 ounces) semi-sweet
  chocolate chips
1 (14-ounce) can EAGLE®
  Brand Sweetened
  Condensed Milk (NOT
  evaporated milk)

1 cup finely ground nuts
1 teaspoon vanilla extract

In small saucepan, over low heat, melt chips with sweetened condensed milk; remove from heat. Stir in nuts and vanilla. In individual 2½-inch foil-lined muffin cups, spread about 2 tablespoons chocolate mixture on bottom and up side to rim of each cup with spoon. Freeze 2 hours or until firm. Before serving, remove foil liners. Store unfilled cups tightly covered in freezer. *Makes about 1½ dozen*

Peanut Butter Ripple Ice Cream

½ cup crunchy peanut butter
¾ cup honey
1 teaspoon orange extract

½ teaspoon ground nutmeg
2 quarts vanilla ice cream

Combine peanut butter, honey, extract and nutmeg. Layer ice cream and peanut butter mixture into metal bowl or other 2 quart freezer container, beginning and ending with the ice cream. Freeze until firm. Scoop or spoon into serving dishes. *Makes about 2 quarts*

Favorite recipe from **Oklahoma Peanut Commission**

Espresso Praline Ice Cream

PRALINE
¾ cup sugar
1 tablespoon plus 2 teaspoons
   water

1½ cups BLUE DIAMOND®
   Sliced Natural Almonds,
   toasted (see Tip below)

ICE CREAM
2 cups whipping cream
2 cups half-and-half
¾ cup sugar
5 egg yolks, beaten
1 tablespoon vanilla extract

1 teaspoon almond extract
2 tablespoons instant espresso
   powder
2 tablespoons brandy

To prepare praline, grease cookie sheet. Mix sugar and water together in heavy saucepan. Over medium-low heat, cook sugar and water until water evaporates and sugar turns golden brown, about 5 minutes. Working rapidly, add almonds and stir until all almonds are lightly coated. Spread immediately on prepared cookie sheet. Cool. Process in food processor or crush with rolling pin until the size of small peas. Reserve.

To prepare ice cream, combine cream, half-and-half and sugar. Cook and stir over medium heat until sugar is dissolved and mixture is hot. Gradually add 1 cup cream mixture to beaten egg yolks, whisking constantly. When mixture is smooth, strain into double boiler. Gradually pour in remaining cream mixture, whisking constantly. Cook over simmering water, stirring until mixture thickens slightly and coats the back of a spoon, about 8 minutes. *Do not boil.* Stir in extracts.

Combine espresso powder and brandy in large bowl. Strain cream mixture into bowl, stirring to dissolve espresso. Cool. Stir in almond praline. Pour into ice cream freezer container. Freeze according to manufacturer's instructions.   *Makes about 1 quart*

Tip: To toast nuts, spread nuts on baking sheet. Bake at 350°F, stirring occasionally 8 to 10 minutes or until lightly browned; cool.

Old-Fashioned Orange Ice Cream

2 cups milk
1 cup sugar
4 eggs, lightly beaten
2 cups (1 pint) whipping cream

1 can (12 ounces) Florida
  frozen concentrate orange
  juice, thawed, undiluted

In top of double boiler, over simmering water, combine milk, sugar and eggs. Cook, stirring constantly, until mixture thickens and coats the back of a spoon. Cool. Stir in cream and orange juice concentrate.

Transfer mixture to ice cream freezer container. Freeze according to manufacturer's directions. Or, turn into 9×5-inch loaf pan; freeze 2 to 3 hours or until almost firm. Turn mixture into bowl; beat until light and fluffy. Return to loaf pan; cover. Freeze 3 to 4 hours or until completely firm. *Makes about 2 quarts*

Favorite recipe from **Florida Department of Citrus**

Frozen Peanut Banana Yogurt

2 tablespoons lemon juice
1½ cups mashed ripe bananas
   (1½ pounds or about
   3 bananas)
1 cup peanut butter

⅓ cup honey
3 (8-ounce) cartons lemon-
   flavored yogurt
½ cup chopped peanuts

Add lemon juice to mashed bananas in small bowl. Combine peanut butter and honey in large bowl; mix in bananas. Add yogurt and chopped peanuts; mix well. Place in ice cream freezer container. Freeze according to manufacturer's instructions. *Makes about 1½ quarts*

REFRIGERATOR-FREEZER METHOD: Pour mixture into 3 ice cube trays or two 9×5-inch loaf pans. Freeze until solid. Break into chunks and beat in large bowl with electric mixer until smooth. Cover; freeze until firm. If mixture becomes too hard, let stand in refrigerator 30 minutes before serving.

Favorite recipe from **Oklahoma Peanut Commission**

Simple Spumoni

Simple Spumoni

2 cups whipping cream
²/₃ cup sweetened condensed
   milk
½ teaspoon rum flavoring

1 can (21 ounces) cherry pie
   filling
½ cup chopped almonds
½ cup miniature chocolate chips

Combine cream, sweetened condensed milk and rum flavoring in large bowl; refrigerate 30 minutes. Beat just until soft peaks form. *Do not overbeat.* Fold in remaining ingredients. Pour into 8×8-inch pan. Cover; freeze about 4 hours or until firm. Scoop out to serve. Garnish as desired. *Makes about 1 quart*

Favorite recipe from **Cherry Marketing Institute, Inc.**

Tangerine Sorbet

½ cup sugar
  1 envelope unflavored gelatin

3 cups fresh Florida tangerine
   juice, divided
1 teaspoon grated tangerine peel

In medium bowl, combine sugar and gelatin. Heat 1 cup tangerine juice to boiling. Add to gelatin and stir until gelatin is completely dissolved. Stir in remaining 2 cups juice and grated peel. Cool. Pour into 9×9-inch pan; cover and freeze. When almost frozen, scrape into large bowl. Beat until smooth, but still frozen. Return to pan; cover and freeze until almost frozen. Scrape into bowl and beat. Spoon into pan; cover and freeze until firm. *Makes about 1 quart*

Favorite recipe from **Florida Department of Citrus**

Fruit Flavor Freeze

Fruit Flavor Freeze

1 package (4-serving size)
  JELL-O® Brand Gelatin,
  any flavor
¾ cup sugar
1 cup boiling water

2 cups milk
1¾ cups (4-ounces) COOL WHIP®
  Whipped Topping, thawed
Assorted cookies, optional

Dissolve gelatin and sugar in boiling water. Stir in milk. (Mixture will appear curdled but will be smooth when frozen.) Pour into 13×9-inch pan. Freeze until ice crystals form 1 inch around edge, about 1 hour.

Spoon gelatin mixture into chilled bowl. Beat until smooth. Blend in whipped topping. Return to pan. Freeze until firm, about 4 hours. Serve with assorted cookies, if desired.   *Makes 10 servings*

Prep time: 15 minutes
Freezing time: 5 hours

White Chocolate Ice Cream

1 cup BLUE DIAMOND® Whole
  Natural Almonds, coarsely
  chopped
1 tablespoon butter
3 cups whipping cream
1 cup milk

4 egg yolks
¾ cup sugar
1 tablespoon vanilla extract
½ cup kirsch
1 cup grated white chocolate

Sauté almonds in butter in skillet over medium heat until crisp; reserve. Combine cream and milk in saucepan; cook over medium heat until skin forms on surface. Beat yolks and sugar with vanilla in medium bowl; gradually add cream mixture, whisking constantly. Strain into double boiler and cook over simmering water, stirring until mixture thickens and lightly coats the back of a spoon, about 10 minutes. *Do not boil.* Remove from heat; add kirsch and white chocolate, stirring until chocolate melts. Cool to room temperature. Add almonds. Pour into ice cream freezer container. Freeze according to manufacturer's instructions.   *Makes 1 quart*

Minted Grapefruit Ice

½ cup plus *1 tablespoon sugar, divided*
1½ *teaspoons unflavored gelatin (½ of envelope)*

½ *cup water*
1 *teaspoon dried mint leaves*
3 *cups Florida grapefruit juice*
1 *egg white**

In small saucepan, mix ½ cup sugar and gelatin. Add water and mint. Let stand 1 minute. Bring to a boil over medium heat, stirring constantly, until gelatin dissolves. Remove from heat. Cover. Let stand 10 minutes.

Pour grapefruit juice into large metal bowl. Strain gelatin mixture through a very fine sieve or several layers of cheese cloth to remove mint leaves. Stir gelatin mixture into grapefruit juice.

Freeze 3 hours or until ice crystals form, 2-inches deep, around edge of bowl. Mix well with wire whisk to break up crystals. Freeze 1½ to 2 hours longer or until firm.

With electric mixer, beat egg white until soft peaks form; add remaining 1 tablespoon sugar, beat until stiff peaks form. Beat grapefruit ice until smooth; fold in beaten egg white. Freeze 1 hour. Stir and freeze until firm.   *Makes 10 to 12 servings*

*Use only grade A clean, uncracked egg.

Favorite recipe from **Florida Department of Citrus**

Blackberry-Lemon Ice Cream

2 *cups fresh or thawed frozen unsweetened blackberries, mashed*
1 *(14-ounce) can EAGLE® Brand Sweetened Condensed Milk (NOT evaporated milk)*

¼ *cup REALEMON® Lemon Juice from Concentrate*
1 *teaspoon grated lemon peel, optional*
3 *cups (1½ pints) BORDEN® or MEADOW GOLD® Half-and-Half*

In large bowl, combine blackberries, sweetened condensed milk, ReaLemon brand and lemon peel if desired. Stir in half-and-half. Pour into ice cream freezer container. Freeze according to manufacturer's instructions. Freeze leftovers.   *Makes about 2 quarts*

Tip: Two cups fresh or thawed frozen unsweetened blueberries or raspberries, mashed, can be substituted for blackberries.

Left to right: Easy Vanilla Ice Cream; Blackberry-Lemon Ice Cream

Easy Vanilla Ice Cream

2 cups (1 pint) BORDEN® or
  MEADOW GOLD®
  Half-and-Half
2 cups (1 pint) BORDEN® or
  MEADOW GOLD®
  Whipping Cream,
  unwhipped

1 (14-ounce) can EAGLE®
  Brand Sweetened
  Condensed Milk (NOT
  evaporated milk)
2 tablespoons vanilla extract

In large bowl, combine ingredients; mix well. Pour into ice cream
freezer container. Freeze according to manufacturer's instructions.
Freeze leftovers.   *Makes about 1½ quarts*

REFRIGERATOR-FREEZER METHOD: Omit half-and-half. Whip
whipping cream. In large bowl, combine sweetened condensed milk and
vanilla; mix well. Fold in whipped cream. Pour into 9×5-inch loaf pan
or other 2-quart container; cover. Freeze 6 hours or until firm. Freeze
leftovers.

Banana Cookie Ice Cream

Banana Cookie Ice Cream

2 ripe DOLE® Bananas, peeled,
   mashed
10 chocolate sandwich cookies,
   finely chopped
1 quart vanilla ice cream,
   softened

¼ cup chocolate syrup
Additional chocolate syrup
DOLE® Banana slices
Maraschino cherries

Fold bananas and cookies into ice cream in large bowl. Pour into 8×8-inch pan. Drizzle with chocolate syrup. Run knife through mixture to make swirls. Cover; freeze until firm.

To serve, scoop into sundae glass. Top with additional chocolate sauce, banana slices and maraschino cherries, if desired.

Makes about 8 servings

Ricotta Gelato

1/2 cup golden raisins
1/4 cup rum
2 cups milk
2/3 cup sugar
4 egg yolks

1 container (15-ounces)
  POLLY-O® Ricotta Cheese
Grated peel of 1 lemon
1 teaspoon vanilla extract

In small bowl, combine raisins and rum. Cover and set aside for several hours or overnight.

In heavy, medium saucepan, combine milk and sugar. Cook over medium-high heat, stirring occasionally, until sugar is dissolved and mixture is hot.

In medium bowl, whisk egg yolks briefly. Gradually whisk half of hot milk mixture into beaten egg yolks. Slowly whisk mixture back into saucepan.

Cook over medium heat, stirring constantly, until custard thickens enough to lightly coat back of spoon, about 8 minutes. *Do not boil.* Immediately pour into bowl and cool slightly.

In blender or food processor, process ricotta until smooth. Gradually blend in cooled custard, lemon peel and vanilla.

Pour mixture into ice cream freezer container. Freeze according to manufacturer's instructions. About halfway through freezing process, stir in raisins and rum.   *Makes about 6 cups*

REFRIGERATOR-FREEZER METHOD: Pour custard mixture in a 13×9×2-inch pan; cover and freeze until slushy, about 2 hours. Transfer to a bowl and beat until smooth. Return ice cream to pan. Cover and freeze until almost solid, about 2 hours. Beat until smooth; stir in raisins and rum. Serve immediately.

Prep time: 20 minutes
Cooking time: 10 minutes
Freezing time: 45 minutes

Left to right: Mint Chocolate Chip Ice Cream; Butter Pecan Ice Cream

Mint Chocolate Chip Ice Cream

1 (14-ounce) can EAGLE®
  Brand Sweetened
  Condensed Milk (NOT
  evaporated milk)
2 teaspoons peppermint extract
  Green food coloring, optional
2 cups (1 pint) BORDEN® or
  MEADOW GOLD®
  Half-and-Half

2 cups (1 pint) BORDEN® or
  MEADOW GOLD®
  Whipping Cream,
  unwhipped
¾ cup mini chocolate chips

In large bowl, combine sweetened condensed milk, extract and food coloring if desired; mix well. Stir in remaining ingredients. Pour into ice cream freezer container. Freeze according to manufacturer's instructions. Freeze leftovers.   *Makes about 1½ quarts*

REFRIGERATOR-FREEZER METHOD: Omit half-and-half; reduce mini chocolate chips to ½ cup. Whip whipping cream. In large bowl, combine sweetened condensed milk, extract and food coloring if desired; mix well. Fold in whipped cream and chocolate chips. Pour into 9×5-inch loaf pan or other 2-quart container; cover. Freeze 6 hours or until firm. Freeze leftovers.

Butter Pecan Ice Cream

1 (14-ounce) can EAGLE®
  Brand Sweetened
  Condensed Milk (NOT
  evaporated milk)
1 to 1½ cups chopped pecans,
  toasted (see Tip page 39)
3 tablespoons butter or
  margarine, melted

1 teaspoon maple flavoring
2 cups (1 pint) BORDEN® or
  MEADOW GOLD®
  Half-and-Half
2 cups (1 pint) BORDEN® or
  MEADOW GOLD®
  Whipping Cream,
  unwhipped

In large bowl, combine sweetened condensed milk, pecans, butter and flavoring; mix well. Stir in remaining ingredients. Pour into ice cream freezer container. Freeze according to manufacturer's instructions. Freeze leftovers.   *Makes about 2 quarts*

REFRIGERATOR-FREEZER METHOD: Omit half-and-half. Whip whipping cream. In large bowl, combine sweetened condensed milk, pecans, butter and flavoring; mix well. Fold in whipped cream. Pour into 9×5-inch loaf pan or other 2-quart container; cover. Freeze 6 hours or until firm. Freeze leftovers.

Pink Champagne Sorbet

1 package (4-serving size)
  JELL-O® Brand Gelatin,
  Strawberry Flavor
1⅓ cups boiling water

1 bottle (187 mL) pink
  champagne
¾ cup light corn syrup
2 egg whites, lightly beaten
  Lime slices, optional

Dissolve gelatin in boiling water. Stir in champagne and corn syrup. Beat in egg whites with wire whisk. Pour into 13×9-inch pan. Freeze until firm, about 2 hours.

Spoon ½ of the gelatin mixture into food processor or blender; cover. Process at high speed until smooth but not melted, about 30 seconds. Pour into 9×5-inch loaf pan. Repeat with remaining mixture; pour over mixture in pan. Cover; freeze until firm, about 6 hours or overnight. Scoop gelatin mixture into dessert or champagne glasses. Garnish with lime slices, if desired.   *Makes 8 servings*

Note: Use only grade A clean eggs with no cracks in shell.

Prep time: 15 minutes
Freezing time: 8 hours

Peach Ice Cream

3 cups (1½ pints) BORDEN® or
MEADOW GOLD®
Half-and-Half
1 (14-ounce) can EAGLE®
Brand Sweetened
Condensed Milk (NOT
evaporated milk)

1 cup puréed or mashed peaches
1 tablespoon vanilla extract
Yellow food coloring, optional

In ice cream freezer container, combine ingredients; mix well. Freeze according to manufacturer's instructions. Freeze leftovers.

Makes about 1½ quarts

REFRIGERATOR-FREEZER METHOD: Omit half-and-half. In large bowl, combine sweetened condensed milk and vanilla; stir in puréed peaches and food coloring if desired. Fold in 2 cups (1 pint) Borden® or Meadow Gold® Whipping Cream, whipped (*do not use non-dairy whipped topping*). Pour into 9×5-inch loaf pan or other 2-quart container; cover. Freeze 6 hours or until firm. Freeze leftovers.

Fresh Berry Ice Cream

3 cups (1½ pints) BORDEN® or
MEADOW GOLD®
Half-and-Half
1 (14-ounce) can EAGLE®
Brand Sweetened
Condensed Milk (NOT
evaporated milk)

1 cup puréed or mashed fresh
berries (raspberries,
strawberries, etc.)
1 tablespoon vanilla extract
Food coloring, optional

In ice cream freezer container, combine ingredients; mix well. Freeze according to manufacturer's instructions. Freeze leftovers.

Makes about 1½ quarts

REFRIGERATOR-FREEZER METHOD: Omit half-and-half. In large bowl, combine sweetened condensed milk and vanilla; stir in puréed or mashed fruit and food coloring if desired. Fold in 2 cups (1 pint) Borden® or Meadow Gold® Whipping Cream, whipped (*do not use non-dairy whipped topping*). Pour into 9×5-inch loaf pan or other 2-quart container; cover. Freeze 6 hours or until firm. Freeze leftovers.

Peach Ice Cream

Fruit Salsa Sundae (page 60)

SAUCES & SUNDAES

Chocolate-Orange Dessert Sauce

1 cup sugar
1 can (5 or 5⅓ ounces)
* evaporated milk*
1 tablespoon light corn syrup
2 squares (1 ounce each)
* unsweetened chocolate or*
* semi-sweet chocolate (for*
* sweeter sauce)*

3 tablespoons BUTTER
* FLAVOR CRISCO®*
1 teaspoon finely grated orange
* peel*
2 teaspoons orange-flavored
* liqueur or ½ teaspoon*
* orange extract*
¼ teaspoon salt

1. Combine sugar, evaporated milk and corn syrup in 1½- or 2-quart saucepan. Heat to a full boil over medium-high heat, stirring constantly. Boil for 1 minute, stirring constantly. Reduce heat to low; add chocolate and stir until smooth.

2. Remove from heat. Blend in Butter Flavor Crisco, orange peel, liqueur and salt. Serve warm over ice cream or cake.   *Makes 1½ cups*

Chocolate-Orange Dessert Sauce

Peanut Caramel Sauce

1 cup firmly packed light brown
   sugar
1 tablespoon flour
1/8 teaspoon salt

1 cup water
1/2 cup peanut butter
1 teaspoon vanilla

In medium saucepan, mix sugar, flour and salt. Stir in water. Cook and stir over low heat until mixture comes to a full rolling boil. Add peanut butter and bring again to a boil, stirring constantly until smooth. Remove from heat. Add vanilla. Serve hot or cold over ice cream.

Makes about 1½ cups

Favorite recipe from **Oklahoma Peanut Commission**

Mocha Walnut Sauce

1 tablespoon TASTER'S
   CHOICE® Instant Coffee
1 tablespoon boiling water
1/2 cup whipping cream
1/2 cup sugar
1/2 cup butter

One 6-oz. pkg. (1 cup)
   NESTLÉ® Toll House®
   semi-sweet chocolate
   morsels
2 egg yolks
3/4 cup chopped walnuts

In measuring cup, dissolve Taster's Choice instant coffee in boiling water; set aside. In heavy-gauge saucepan, combine cream and sugar. Bring just to boil, stirring constantly, over medium heat. Add butter, Nestlé Toll House semi-sweet chocolate morsels and coffee; stir until smooth. Remove from heat. In small bowl, beat egg yolks. Gradually stir in 2 tablespoons chocolate mixture; mix well. Return to chocolate mixture in saucepan. Cook over low heat, stirring constantly, for 3 minutes; remove from heat. Stir in walnuts. Serve warm over ice cream. Cover and store in refrigerator.*

Makes 2¼ cups sauce

*Reheat sauce in top of double boiler over hot (not boiling) water before using *or* microwave on HIGH about 1 minute for each 1 cup sauce.

Peach Melba Parfaits

Peach Melba Parfaits

1 (10-ounce) package frozen
   red raspberries in syrup,
   thawed
¼ cup red currant jelly
1 tablespoon cornstarch

½ (½-gallon carton) BORDEN®
   or MEADOW GOLD®
   Peach Premium Frozen
   Yogurt
⅔ cup granola or natural cereal

Drain raspberries, reserving ⅔ cup syrup. In small saucepan, combine reserved syrup, jelly and cornstarch. Cook and stir until slightly thickened and glossy. Cool. Stir in raspberries. In parfait or wine glasses, layer raspberry sauce, frozen yogurt then granola; repeat. Freeze. Remove from freezer 5 to 10 minutes before serving. Garnish as desired. Freeze leftovers. *Makes 6 to 8 parfaits*

Pineapple Orange Sauce

1 can (20 ounces) DOLE®
   Pineapple Chunks in juice,
   undrained
Juice and grated peel from
   1 DOLE® Orange

1 tablespoon cornstarch
1 tablespoon sugar
1 teaspoon ground ginger

Combine pineapple, ½ cup orange juice and 1 teaspoon orange peel with remaining ingredients in saucepan.

Cook, stirring, until sauce boils and thickens. Cool. Serve over ice cream, frozen yogurt, pancakes or waffles. *Makes 8 servings*

Prep time: 5 minutes
Cooking time: 5 minutes

Top to bottom: Chocolate Peanut Butter Ice Cream Sauce; Quick Butterscotch Sauce; Luscious Chocolate Almond Sauce

Chocolate Peanut Butter Ice Cream Sauce

One 11½-oz. pkg. (2 cups)
  NESTLÉ® Toll House®
  milk chocolate morsels

¼ cup peanut butter
⅓ cup milk

In small heavy-gauge saucepan, combine Nestlé Toll House milk chocolate morsels, peanut butter and milk. Cook over very low heat, stirring until chocolate melts and mixture is smooth. Serve warm over ice cream. Refrigerate leftover sauce. Reheat sauce over low heat, stirring until smooth.   *Makes about 1½ cups*

Quick Butterscotch Sauce

One 12-oz. pkg. (2 cups)
  NESTLÉ® Toll House®
  butterscotch flavored
  morsels

⅔ cup whipping cream

In small heavy-gauge saucepan, combine Nestlé Toll House butterscotch flavored morsels and cream. Cook over low heat, stirring until morsels are melted and mixture is smooth. Serve warm over ice cream. Refrigerate leftover sauce. Reheat sauce over low heat stirring until smooth.   *Makes about 1½ cups*

Luscious Chocolate Almond Sauce

1 cup (half of 12-oz. pkg.)
  NESTLÉ® Toll House®
  semi-sweet chocolate mini-
  morsels
¼ cup whipping cream
2 tablespoons (¼ stick) butter

⅛ teaspoon salt
¼ cup almonds, coarsely
  chopped and toasted (see
  Tip page 39)
2 tablespoons almond flavored
  liqueur

In heavy-gauge saucepan over low heat, combine Nestlé Toll House semi-sweet mini-morsels, cream, butter and salt, stirring until smooth; remove from heat. Stir in almonds and liqueur; cool slightly. Serve warm over ice cream. Refrigerate leftover sauce. Reheat sauce over low heat, stirring until smooth.   *Makes about 1 cup*

Butter Rum Sundaes

1 cup firmly packed light brown
  sugar
1/3 cup BUTTER FLAVOR
  CRISCO®
1/2 cup dark corn syrup

1/4 cup milk
1 to 2 teaspoons imitation rum
  flavoring
Vanilla ice cream

1. Blend brown sugar, Butter Flavor Crisco and corn syrup in 1-quart saucepan. Cook and stir over medium heat until mixture comes to a boil. Boil 1 minute. Remove from heat. Gradually blend in milk until smooth. Stir in flavoring.

2. Cool until warm. Stir well. Serve over vanilla ice cream. Cover and refrigerate any leftover sauce. Reheat over low heat stirring constantly before serving.   *Makes 6 to 8 sundaes (1 1/2 cups sauce)*

Milk Chocolate Mallow Fudge Sauce

One 11 1/2-oz. pkg. (2 cups)
  NESTLÉ® Toll House®
  milk chocolate morsels
2 cups miniature
  marshmallows

2/3 cup evaporated milk
3 tablespoons butter
1 teaspoon vanilla extract

Combine in top of double boiler over hot (not boiling) water, Nestlé Toll House milk chocolate morsels, marshmallows, evaporated milk and butter. Stir until morsels and marshmallows are melted and mixture is smooth. Remove from heat; stir in vanilla. Serve warm over ice cream. Cover and store in refrigerator.*   *Makes about 2 1/2 cups sauce*

*Reheat sauce in top of double boiler over hot (not boiling) water before using *or* microwave on HIGH about 1 minute for each 1 cup sauce.

Hot Peanut Fudge Sundae

1 package (6 ounces) semi-
  sweet chocolate chips
3/4 cup evaporated milk
1/2 cup peanut butter

1/2 cup marshmallow creme
1 quart vanilla ice cream
1/2 cup chopped roasted peanuts

Melt chocolate in double boiler or in saucepan over very low heat. Add evaporated milk, peanut butter and marshmallow creme. Beat until thoroughly combined. Scoop ice cream into 6 sundae dishes. Ladle on warm sauce; garnish with peanuts.

Makes 6 sundaes (about 2 cups sauce)

Favorite recipe from **Oklahoma Peanut Commission**

Chocolate Peppermint Sauce

¼ cup (½ stick) butter
2 squares (1 ounce each)
   unsweetened chocolate
1⅓ cups sugar
⅛ teaspoon salt

⅔ cup light cream or half-and-half
½ teaspoon vanilla extract
½ cup whipping cream, whipped
½ cup coarsely chopped peppermint candy

Melt butter and chocolate in heavy saucepan over low heat, stirring occasionally. Remove from heat; stir in sugar and salt gradually, mixing until well combined. (Mixture will be thick and dry). Gradually stir in cream and vanilla. Return to heat. Cook over low heat until sugar is dissolved, about 5 minutes. Cool. Stir in whipped cream and candy. Refrigerate; serve cold over ice cream.

Makes 3 cups

Favorite recipe from **American Dairy Association**

Pineapple Strawberry Sauce

2 cans (8 ounces each) DOLE®
   Crushed Pineapple in juice,
   undrained
1 package (10 ounces) frozen
   strawberries, thawed,
   puréed

¼ cup sugar
4 teaspoons cornstarch
   Grated peel and juice from
   1 DOLE® Lemon

Combine pineapple, strawberries, sugar, cornstarch, 1 teaspoon lemon peel and 1 tablespoon lemon juice in large saucepan. Cook, stirring, until sauce boils and thickens. Cool. Serve over ice cream.

Makes 8 servings

Prep time: 5 minutes
Cooking time: 5 minutes

Fruit Salsa Sundaes

4 (6-inch) flour tortillas
1½ cups diced peeled peaches
1½ cups diced strawberries
2 tablespoons sugar
1 tablespoon finely chopped
   crystallized ginger

½ teaspoon grated lime peel
4 scoops (4 ounces each)
   DREYER'S/EDY'S GRAND
   LIGHT® Vanilla
Sprigs of fresh mint, for
   garnish

Preheat oven to 350°F. Soften tortillas according to package directions. Press each one down in ungreased 10-ounce custard cup. Bake 10 to 15 minutes or until crisp. Set aside to cool.

Combine peaches, strawberries, sugar, ginger and lime peel in large bowl; mix gently until well blended. To assemble, remove tortillas from custard cups. Place each tortilla shell on dessert plate and fill with 1 scoop of Grand Light. Spoon equal portions of fruit salsa over tops. Garnish with mint sprigs. *Makes 4 servings*

Chocolate Lover's Ice Cream Sauce

½ cup HERSHEY'S® Syrup
30 HERSHEY'S KISSES®
   chocolate, unwrapped

Any flavor ice cream

In small heavy saucepan combine syrup and Kisses; stir lightly. Cook over very low heat, stirring constantly, until Kisses are melted and mixture is smooth. Remove from heat. Spoon sauce over ice cream. Serve immediately. Cover and refrigerate leftover sauce.

Makes about 1 cup sauce

To reheat: In large bowl containing about 1 inch very hot water place smaller bowl containing sauce. Allow to stand several minutes to soften; stir to desired consistency.

MICROWAVE DIRECTIONS: In small microwave-safe bowl combine syrup and Kisses; stir lightly. Microwave at HIGH (100%) 15 seconds; stir. Microwave additional 30 seconds; stir until Kisses are melted and mixture is smooth. If necessary, microwave additional 15 seconds or as needed to melt Kisses.

To reheat: Microwave at HIGH a few seconds at a time; stir. Repeat until warm.

Fruit Salsa Sundae

Peanut Butter Sauce

1 (14-ounce) can EAGLE®
    Brand Sweetened
    Condensed Milk (NOT
    evaporated milk)
¼ to ⅓ cup peanut butter

⅓ cup chopped peanuts,
    optional
1 teaspoon vanilla extract
½ teaspoon ground cinnamon

In heavy saucepan, over low heat, combine sweetened condensed milk and peanut butter; cook and stir until well blended. Remove from heat; add remaining ingredients. Serve warm over ice cream. Refrigerate leftovers.   *Makes about 2 cups*

To Reheat: In small heavy saucepan, combine desired amount of sauce with small amount of water. Over low heat, stir constantly until heated through.

MICROWAVE DIRECTIONS: In 1-quart glass measure with handle, combine sweetened condensed milk and peanut butter. Cook on 100% power (HIGH) 2½ to 3½ minutes, stirring after each minute. Proceed as above.

Hot Fudge Sauce

1 cup (6 ounces) semi-sweet
    chocolate chips or
    4 (1-ounce) squares semi-
    sweet chocolate
2 tablespoons margarine or
    butter

1 (14-ounce) can EAGLE®
    Brand Sweetened
    Condensed Milk (NOT
    evaporated milk)
2 tablespoons water
1 teaspoon vanilla extract

In heavy saucepan, over medium heat, melt chips and margarine with sweetened condensed milk and water. Cook and stir constantly until thickened, about 5 minutes. Add vanilla. Serve warm over ice cream or as a fruit dipping sauce. Refrigerate leftovers.   *Makes about 2 cups*

To Reheat: In small heavy saucepan, combine desired amount of sauce with small amount of water. Over low heat, stir constantly until heated through.

MICROWAVE DIRECTIONS: In 1-quart glass measure with handle, combine all ingredients. Cook on 100% power (HIGH) 3 to 3½ minutes, stirring after each minute. Proceed as above.

Top to bottom: Peanut Butter Sauce;
Hot Fudge Sauce; Coconut Pecan Sauce

Coconut Pecan Sauce

1 (14-ounce) can EAGLE®
    Brand Sweetened
    Condensed Milk (NOT
    evaporated milk)
2 egg yolks, beaten

¼ cup margarine or butter
½ cup flaked coconut
½ cup chopped pecans
1 teaspoon vanilla extract

In heavy saucepan, combine sweetened condensed milk, egg yolks and margarine. Over medium heat, cook and stir until thickened and bubbly, about 8 minutes. Stir in remaining ingredients. Serve warm over ice cream or cake. Refrigerate leftovers.   *Makes about 2 cups*

To Reheat: In small heavy saucepan, combine desired amount of sauce with small amount of water. Over low heat, stir constantly until heated through.

MICROWAVE DIRECTIONS: In 1-quart glass measure with handle, combine sweetened condensed milk, egg yolks and margarine. Cook on 70% power (MEDIUM-HIGH) 4 to 5 minutes, stirring after 3 minutes. Proceed as above.

Light Bananas Romanoff

Light Bananas Romanoff

½ cup strawberry jam
1 tablespoon orange liqueur or
   frozen orange juice
   concentrate, thawed
2 firm, medium DOLE®
   Bananas, peeled

1 pint lowfat strawberry or
   vanilla frozen yogurt or ice
   cream
¼ cup DOLE® Sliced Almonds,
   toasted (see Tip page 39)

Combine jam and liqueur in medium bowl. Slice bananas; fold into jam mixture. Serve bananas spooned over scoops of frozen yogurt. Sprinkle with almonds.   *Makes 4 servings*

Prep time: 5 minutes

Mint Fudge Sauce

1 cup (6 ounces) semi-sweet
   chocolate chips
4 ounces chocolate coated mint
   cream patties, broken up

½ cup undiluted *CARNATION*®
   Evaporated Milk
½ cup light corn syrup
1 tablespoon butter

In medium saucepan, combine chocolate chips, mint patties, evaporated milk and corn syrup. Cook over medium-low heat, stirring constantly, until all ingredients are melted. Remove from heat. Stir in butter until melted. Serve warm over ice cream. Store covered in refrigerator. Reheat sauce over low heat stirring constantly.   *Makes 2 cups*

Kahlúa®-Colada Parfaits

8 purchased macaroon cookies	8 teaspoons rum
½ cup KAHLÚA®	¼ cup shredded coconut, toasted
1 quart vanilla ice cream	(see Tip page 18)
1 (20-ounce) can crushed	Fresh pineapple wedges,
pineapple in juice,	optional
thoroughly drained	

In each of four parfait glasses or 12-ounce wine glasses, crumble 1 cookie. Sprinkle each with 1 tablespoon Kahlúa. Top with ¼ cup ice cream in each glass, then spoon layer of pineapple over ice cream and sprinkle each with 1 teaspoon rum. Repeat layers using remaining cookies, Kahlúa, ice cream, pineapple and rum, ending with the ice cream. Sprinkle with toasted coconut and garnish with pineapple wedges, if desired. Serve immediately.   *Makes 4 servings*

Easy Peanut Butter Sauce

½ cup chunky peanut butter	2 tablespoons milk
½ cup light or dark corn syrup	

In small bowl, stir peanut butter, corn syrup and milk until well-blended. Serve over ice cream. Store in tightly covered container in refrigerator. Reheat sauce over low heat stirring constantly.

Makes 1 cup

Chocolate Chip-Peanut Butter Sauce: Follow recipe for Easy Peanut Butter Sauce. Add ½ cup mini semi-sweet chocolate chips.

Makes 1⅓ cups

Fruit and Honey-Peanut Butter Sauce: Follow recipe for Easy Peanut Butter Sauce. Reduce corn syrup to ¼ cup. Add ½ cup coarsely chopped apple or banana, ¼ cup honey and ⅛ teaspoon ground cinnamon.   *Makes 1½ cups*

Peanut Butter and Jelly Sauce: Follow recipe for Easy Peanut Butter Sauce. Omit milk. Add ½ cup grape or strawberry jelly, melted.

Makes about 1⅓ cups

Favorite Recipe from **Oklahoma Peanut Commission**

Frozen Fruity Bars;
Frozen Pudding Bars (page 68)

COOL KIDS' FUN

Clown Cupcakes

1 package DUNCAN HINES®
    Yellow Cake Mix
12 scoops vanilla ice cream
1 package (12 count) sugar ice
    cream cones

1 container (7 ounces)
    refrigerated aerosol
    whipped cream
Assorted candies for eyes,
    nose and mouth

1. Preheat oven to 350°F. Place 2½-inch paper liners in 24 muffin cups.

2. Prepare, bake and cool cupcakes following package directions. To assemble each clown, remove paper from cupcake. Place top-side down on serving plate. Top with a scoop of ice cream. Place cone on ice cream for hat. Spray whipped cream around bottom of cupcake for collar. Spray three small dots up front of cone. Sprinkle whipped cream with assorted colored decors. Use candies to make clown's face.

Makes 12 clown cupcakes

Note: This recipe makes 24 cupcakes: 12 to make into "clowns" and 12 to freeze for later use. Cupcakes will keep frozen in airtight container for up to 6 weeks.

Tip: For easier preparation, make the ice cream balls ahead of time. Scoop out balls of ice cream, place on baking sheet or in bowl and return to freezer to firm.

Clown Cupcakes

Frozen Fruity Bars;
Frozen Pudding Bars

Frozen Fruity Bars

1 package (4-serving size)
JELL-O® Brand Gelatin, any
flavor

½ cup sugar
2 cups boiling water
2 cups cold water

Dissolve gelatin and sugar in boiling water. Add cold water. Pour into pop molds or paper or plastic cups. Freeze until almost firm, about 2 hours. Insert wooden stick or spoon into each cup. Freeze until firm, about 8 hours or overnight.   *Makes 8 pops*

Prep time: 15 minutes
Freezing time: 8 hours

Frozen Pudding Bars

1 package (4-serving size)
JELL-O® Instant Pudding
and Pie filling, any flavor

2 cups cold milk

Prepare pudding mix with milk as directed on package. Pour into pop molds or paper or plastic cups. Insert wooden stick or spoon into each cup. Freeze until firm, about 5 hours.   *Makes 6 pops*

Prep time: 10 minutes
Freezing time: 5 hours

Chocolate-Covered Banana Pops

3 ripe, large bananas
9 wooden ice cream sticks or
skewers
2 cups (12-ounce package)
HERSHEY'S® Semi-Sweet
Chocolate Chips

2 tablespoons shortening
1½ cups coarsely chopped
unsalted, roasted peanuts

Peel bananas; cut each into thirds. Insert wooden stick into each banana piece; place on wax paper-covered tray. Cover; freeze until firm.

In top of double boiler over hot, not boiling, water melt chocolate chips and shortening. Remove bananas from freezer just before dipping. Dip each piece into warm chocolate, covering completely; allow excess to drip off. Immediately roll in peanuts. Cover; return to freezer. Serve frozen.

Makes 9 pops

Let-the-Good-Times-Roll Pinwheels

1 quart softened ice cream, any
flavor
1½ cups TEDDY GRAHAMS®
Graham Snacks, any flavor,
divided
1 quart softened sherbet, any
flavor

Chocolate fudge sauce,
prepared whipped topping
and colored sprinkles, for
garnish

Spread ice cream evenly on waxed paper-lined 15½×10½×1-inch baking pan; sprinkle with 1¼ cups Teddy Grahams. Freeze until firm, about 40 minutes. Spread sherbet over Teddy Grahams layer. Freeze until firm, about 2 to 3 hours.

Beginning at short end, roll up frozen layers jelly-roll fashion, removing waxed paper; place roll on serving dish. Cover and freeze at least 1 hour.

To serve, garnish with chocolate fudge sauce, whipped topping, sprinkles and remaining ¼ cup Teddy Grahams. Slice and serve immediately.

Makes 12 servings

Dish of Dirt

14 OREO® Chocolate Sandwich
    Cookies, finely crushed
    (about 1 cup crumbs)
1 pint chocolate ice cream

¼ cup chocolate-flavored syrup
    Gummy worms and prepared
    whipped topping, for
    garnish

In each of 4 dessert dishes, place 2 tablespoons cookie crumbs. Top each with ½ cup ice cream, remaining 2 tablespoons cookie crumbs and 1 tablespoon syrup. Garnish with gummy worms and whipped topping.

Makes 4 servings

Frozen Celebration Cake

8 finger-shaped creme-filled
    chocolate snack cakes, cut
    lengthwise
½ gallon BORDEN® or
    MEADOW GOLD® Ice
    Cream, any flavor, slightly
    softened

1 (8-ounce) container frozen
    non-dairy whipped topping,
    thawed
    Chocolate covered round
    snack cakes, optional
    Licorice string and tube
    decorator icing, optional

Line 13×9-inch pan with 22-inch piece of aluminum foil, extending foil over ends of pan. Arrange cut snack cakes in bottom of pan. Spoon ice cream into prepared pan. Spread whipped topping evenly over ice cream. For "balloon" decoration, arrange round snack cakes on top using licorice as balloon strings. Cover. Freeze overnight or until firm. Lifting ends of foil, remove from pan; peel off foil. Garnish with icing. Freeze leftovers.

Makes 1 (13×9-inch cake)

Chocolate Chip Ice Cream Sandwiches

1 (14-ounce) can EAGLE®
    Brand Sweetened
    Condensed Milk (NOT
    evaporated milk)
2 tablespoons vanilla extract
2 cups (1 pint) BORDEN® or
    MEADOW GOLD®
    Whipping Cream, whipped
    (do not use non-dairy
    whipped topping)

¾ cup mini chocolate chips
24 to 30 chocolate chip or
    chocolate wafer cookies

In large bowl, combine sweetened condensed milk and vanilla; mix well. Fold in whipped cream and chips. Pour into 9×5-inch loaf pan or other 2-quart container; cover. Freeze 6 hours or until firm. Scoop about ¼ cup ice cream into bottom of 1 cookie; top with another cookie, top side up. Press gently. Wrap tightly with plastic wrap. Repeat for remaining sandwiches. Store in freezer.

Makes about 12 to 15 servings

Dish of Dirt

Banana Bonanza Ice Cream

Banana Bonanza Ice Cream

2 cups milk
2 cups whipping cream
2 eggs, beaten
1¼ cups sugar

2 extra-ripe, medium DOLE®
   Bananas, peeled
½ teaspoon vanilla extract
¼ teaspoon salt
⅛ teaspoon ground nutmeg

In saucepan, combine milk, cream, eggs and sugar. Cook and stir over low heat until mixture thickens slightly and coats the back of a spoon. Cool to room temperature.

Pureé bananas in blender (1 cup). Combine cooled custard, bananas, vanilla, salt and nutmeg. Pour into ice cream freezer container. Freeze according to manufacturer's directions.   *Makes 16 servings*

Fruit & Ice Cream Pizza

½ (20-ounce) package
   refrigerated cookie dough,
   any flavor
1 quart BORDEN® or
   MEADOW GOLD® Ice
   Cream, any flavor, softened

Assorted cut-up fresh or
   canned fruits
½ cup pineapple or strawberry
   ice cream topping

Preheat oven to 350°F. Press cookie dough into greased 12-inch pizza pan or into 12-inch circle on greased baking sheet; bake 12 to 14 minutes. Cool. Spoon ice cream onto crust; freeze until firm. Top with fruit and drizzle with topping.   *Makes 1 (12-inch) pizza*

Watermelon Bombe

1 quart mint chocolate chip or
   pistachio ice cream,
   softened
1½ pints vanilla ice cream,
   softened

1 quart strawberry ice cream,
   softened
2 tablespoons semi-sweet
   chocolate pieces

Chill 2½-quart mixing bowl in freezer at least 30 minutes. Line bottom and side of bowl with mint ice cream using broad, flat ice cream spade or spoon. Work quickly; do not let ice cream melt. Freeze until firm. Layer vanilla ice cream over mint leaving center hollow. Freeze until firm. Mix chocolate pieces through strawberry ice cream. Pack into center. Cover with foil. Freeze several hours or overnight. To unmold, quickly dip bowl in cold water. Run metal spatula around edge of bowl. Invert onto chilled serving dish. Return to freezer up to 1 hour before serving. Let stand at room temperature 15 minutes before slicing.

Makes 10 to 12 servings

Favorite recipe from **American Dairy Association**

Peanut Rocky Road

1 cup cocktail peanuts, chopped
1 cup semi-sweet chocolate
   chips
2 cups miniature marshmallows

3 pints vanilla ice cream, cut up
1½ cups peanut butter, divided

In large bowl, toss together peanuts, chocolate chips and marshmallows; set aside. In electric mixer bowl, beat ice cream until smooth. Spoon half of the ice cream into chilled 8-inch square pan; spread evenly. Swirl ¾ cup peanut butter into ice cream in pan. If ice cream is too soft to swirl in peanut butter return to freezer for a short time. Sprinkle half of the peanut-marshmallow mixture over ice cream. Spread remaining ice cream over peanut-marshmallow mixture; swirl in remaining ¾ cup peanut butter. Sprinkle remaining peanut-marshmallow mixture over top; press lightly. Freeze until set. Cut into 2×2½-inch bars.

Makes about 12 servings

Favorite recipe from **Oklahoma Peanut Commission**

Frozen Peanut Pops

1 pint vanilla ice cream
1 cup peanut butter
1/2 cup milk

3/4 cup peanuts, chopped
3/4 cup chocolate fudge topping

In large bowl beat ice cream until soft. Beat in peanut butter alternately with milk. To assemble, place 1 tablespoon chopped peanuts in bottom of each of six 5-ounce paper cups. Spread 1 tablespoon fudge topping over nuts and spoon in 1/4 cup peanut ice cream. Repeat layers ending with ice cream. Insert wooden stick in center of each; freeze until firm. To serve, remove paper cup.   *Makes 6 pops*

Favorite recipe from **Oklahoma Peanut Commission**

Teddy Peanut Butter Swirl Pie

2 cups TEDDY GRAHAMS®
   Graham Snacks, any flavor,
   divided
1 (8-inch) prepared cookie
   crumb pie crust

1/2 cup creamy peanut butter
1 quart vanilla ice milk,
   softened
1/4 cup PLANTERS® Dry Roasted
   Peanuts, chopped

Place 1/2 cup Teddy Grahams in bottom of prepared pie crust. Heat peanut butter over low heat until smooth and pourable, drizzle 1/4 cup over cookies in crust. Fold 1 cup Teddy Grahams into ice milk; spread into pie crust. Drizzle remaining peanut butter over pie; quickly swirl with knife to create a marbled effect. Top with remaining 1/2 cup Teddy Grahams and chopped peanuts. Cover and freeze until firm, about 4 hours.   *Makes 6 servings*

Peanut Butter Ice Cream Sandwiches

1/3 cup peanut butter
1/4 cup packed brown sugar
1/4 cup margarine or butter,
   melted

4 cups Corn CHEX® brand
   cereal, crushed to 1 1/2 cups
1 quart vanilla ice cream,
   softened

Butter 8-inch square baking pan. Combine peanut butter, sugar and margarine, stirring until smooth. Mix in cereal until well blended. Reserve 3/4 cup cereal mixture; press remainder onto bottom of prepared pan. Chill 30 minutes. Spread ice cream over cereal mixture. Top with reserved cereal mixture, pressing lightly.

Freeze until firm, 6 hours or overnight. Cut into squares. Serve plain or with ice cream topping.   *Makes 9 servings*

Brownie Mint Sundae Square

Brownie Mint Sundae Squares

1 (21.5- or 23.6-ounce)
  package fudge brownie mix
¾ cup coarsely chopped walnuts,
  optional
1 (14-ounce) can EAGLE®
  Brand Sweetened
  Condensed Milk (NOT
  evaporated milk)

2 teaspoons peppermint extract
  Green food coloring, optional
2 cups (1 pint) BORDEN® or
  MEADOW GOLD®
  Whipping Cream, whipped
½ cup mini chocolate chips
  Hot Fudge Sauce (see
  page 62)

Prepare brownie mix as package directs; stir in walnuts. Turn into
aluminum foil-lined and greased 13×9-inch baking pan. Bake as
directed. Cool thoroughly. In large bowl, combine sweetened condensed
milk, extract and food coloring if desired. Fold in whipped cream and
chips. Pour over brownie layer. Cover; freeze 6 hours or until firm. To
serve, lift from pan with foil; cut into squares. Serve with Hot Fudge
Sauce or chocolate ice cream topping if desired. Freeze leftovers.

Makes 10 to 12 servings

Chocolate Tortoni (page 80)

FROZEN FINALES

Brownie Alaska

1 package DUNCAN HINES®
  Chocolate Lover's Double
  Fudge Brownie Mix
½ gallon brick strawberry ice
  cream

6 egg whites
2 cups marshmallow creme

1. Preheat oven to 350°F. Line 13×9×2-inch pan with foil.

2. Prepare, bake and cool brownie mix following package directions.

3. Invert brownie onto cookie sheet. Remove foil and cut in half crosswise so each half measures 8½×6 inches. Cut brick ice cream in half horizontally. Place each half on brownie halves. Trim brownie even with ice cream, if desired. Chill in freezer.

4. For meringue, preheat oven to 475°F. Beat egg whites until soft peaks form. Add marshmallow creme, ¼ cup at a time. Beat well after each addition. Beat until stiff peaks form. Divide between two brownie halves. Spread over top and sides sealing edges completely. Bake at 475°F for 2 to 3 minutes or until meringue has browned. Serve immediately.   *Makes 2 brownie Alaskas, 8 to 10 servings each*

Tip: For delicious variations, try different ice creams such as mint chocolate chip, peppermint or chocolate.

Brownie Alaska

Easy Chocolate Berry Charlotte

Easy Chocolate Berry Charlotte

CAKE

½ cup all-purpose flour
¼ teaspoon baking powder
¼ teaspoon salt
3 eggs
½ cup granulated sugar

1 teaspoon vanilla extract
2 tablespoons vegetable oil
    Confectioners' sugar
1 cup strawberry jam

FILLING

3 foil-wrapped bars (6 oz.)
    NESTLÉ® semi-sweet
    chocolate baking bars
1 cup whipping cream

4 to 6 cups strawberry ice
    cream, softened
    Whipped cream
    Fresh sliced strawberries

For cake, preheat oven to 350°F. Grease 15½×10½-inch jelly-roll pan.
Line bottom with waxed paper. In small bowl, combine flour, baking
powder and salt; set aside.

In large mixer bowl at medium-high speed, beat eggs, granulated sugar
and vanilla extract for 4 minutes until thick and pale yellow. Beat in oil
until well combined. Gradually beat in flour mixture. Spread into
prepared pan.

Bake 13 to 16 minutes, until golden. Immediately invert onto towel
sprinkled with confectioners' sugar. Peel off waxed paper. Starting from
long side, roll warm cake, jelly-roll style with towel inside. Cool cake,
seam side down, on wire rack.

Unroll cake and remove towel. Spread strawberry jam evenly over cake
to within ½-inch of edges. Roll up cake. Wrap tightly in foil and freeze
2 hours.

For filling, in small saucepan over low heat, melt semi-sweet chocolate baking bars with cream, stirring until smooth. Remove from heat; cool completely.

Slice jelly roll into ½-inch slices. Tightly line bottom and sides of 2½-quart bowl or 6-cup charlotte mold with cake slices. Spoon one third of ice cream into lined mold. Spread half of filling over ice cream. Repeat layers; top with remaining ice cream. Cover with plastic wrap; freeze until firm or up to 1 week.

To serve, remove plastic wrap; dip mold into bowl of warm water for 15 to 20 seconds. Invert mold onto serving platter; remove mold. Let stand at room temperature 15 minutes until slightly softened. Garnish with whipped cream and strawberries. *Makes 8 to 10 servings*

Pineapple with Caramel Sauce & Pralines

PRALINES
½ cup sugar
2 tablespoons water

½ cup pecans, toasted
(see Tip page 39)

CARAMEL SAUCE
1 cup sugar
½ cup margarine
½ cup half-and-half

1 DOLE® Fresh Pineapple
1 pint vanilla ice cream

For Pralines, cook sugar and water in small saucepan over low heat, stirring constantly until sugar browns and caramelizes. Stir in nuts. Pour onto greased baking sheet. Cool. Break into pieces.

For Caramel Sauce, add sugar to 10-inch heavy skillet. Cook over medium heat, stirring until sugar melts and turns light brown. Remove from heat. Add margarine; stir until melted. Return to low heat. Gradually stir in half-and-half. Cook, stirring, until smooth.

Twist crown from pineapple. Cut pineapple in half lengthwise. Cut fruit from shells with knife. Lay pineapple on flat side. Cut in thin slices.

For each dessert, arrange 4 pineapple slices on dessert plate. Place 3 small scoops ice cream on plate. Spoon hot Caramel Sauce over. Top with Pralines. *Makes 8 servings*

Chocolate Tortoni

1 cup chilled whipping cream
1/2 cup chilled HERSHEY'S®
    Syrup
1/4 cup almond macaroon crumbs
    or vanilla wafer crumbs
1/4 cup plus 2 tablespoons
    chopped almonds, toasted
    and divided (see Tip
    page 39)

1/4 cup chopped maraschino
    cherries, drained
1 1/2 tablespoons rum or
    1/2 teaspoon rum flavoring
    Maraschino cherries, optional

In small mixer bowl, beat whipping cream until stiff; gently fold in syrup. Stir in macaroon crumbs, 1/4 cup chopped almonds, chopped maraschino cherries and rum. Divide mixture among 4 dessert dishes; cover and freeze until firm, about 4 hours. Just before serving, sprinkle with remaining 2 tablespoons chopped almonds. Garnish with maraschino cherries, if desired.

Makes 4 servings

Frozen Chocolate Banana Loaf

1 1/2 cups chocolate wafer cookie
    crumbs (about 30 wafers)
1/4 cup sugar
3 tablespoons margarine or
    butter, melted
1 (14-ounce) can EAGLE®
    Brand Sweetened
    Condensed Milk (NOT
    evaporated milk)

2/3 cup chocolate-flavored syrup
2 small ripe bananas, mashed
    (3/4 cup)
2 cups (1 pint) BORDEN® or
    MEADOW GOLD®
    Whipping Cream, whipped
    (do not use non-dairy
    whipped topping)

Line 9×5-inch loaf pan with aluminum foil, extending foil above sides of pan; butter foil. Combine crumbs, sugar and margarine; press firmly on bottom and halfway up sides of prepared pan. In large bowl, combine sweetened condensed milk, syrup and bananas; mix well. Fold in whipped cream. Pour into prepared pan; cover. Freeze 6 hours or until firm. To serve, remove from pan; peel off foil. Garnish as desired. Slice to serve. Freeze leftovers.

Makes 8 to 10 servings

Chocolate Tortoni

Frozen Amaretto Torte

Frozen Amaretto Torte

1 (8½-ounce) package
   chocolate wafers, finely
   crushed (2½ cups crumbs)
½ cup slivered almonds, toasted
   and chopped (see Tip
   page 39)
⅓ cup margarine or butter,
   melted
1 (6-ounce) package
   butterscotch flavored chips
   (1 cup)

1 (14-ounce) can EAGLE®
   Brand Sweetened
   Condensed Milk (NOT
   evaporated milk)
1 (16-ounce) container
   BORDEN® or MEADOW
   GOLD® Sour Cream
⅓ cup amaretto liqueur
1 cup (½ pint) BORDEN® or
   MEADOW GOLD®
   Whipping Cream, whipped

Combine crumbs, almonds and margarine. Reserving 1¼ cups crumb mixture, press remainder firmly on bottom of 9-inch springform pan. In small saucepan, over medium heat, melt chips with sweetened condensed milk. In large bowl, combine sour cream and amaretto; stir in butterscotch mixture. Fold in whipped cream. Pour half the cream mixture over prepared crust; top with 1 cup reserved crumb mixture, then remaining cream mixture. Top with remaining ¼ cup crumb mixture; cover. Freeze 6 hours or until firm. Garnish as desired. Freeze leftovers.

Makes 12 to 15 servings

Banana Split Bombe

2 pints strawberry ice cream
1½ pints chocolate ice cream
1 pint vanilla ice cream,*
   slightly softened
1 cup puréed bananas
   (about 2 medium)*

¼ teaspoon lemon juice*
Whipped cream
Strawberries
Banana slices

Chill 7-cup mold in freezer. Using an ice cream spade or large spoon, pack ¾-inch layer of strawberry ice cream over bottom and up side of chilled mold. Freeze until firm. Spoon layer of chocolate ice cream over strawberry shell; pack firmly. Freeze until firm. Combine vanilla ice cream, puréed bananas and lemon juice. Pack into center of chocolate shell. Cover and freeze at least 6 hours or overnight.

To unmold, dip mold in lukewarm water just to rim for a few seconds. Loosen ice cream from mold with thin metal spatula. Invert onto chilled serving plate. Return to freezer until firm. To serve, pipe whipped cream in strips up side of bombe. Arrange strawberries and banana slices around base.   *Makes 10 to 12 servings*

*One pint banana ice cream may be substituted for vanilla ice cream, puréed bananas and lemon juice.

Favorite recipe from **American Dairy Association**

Frozen Chocolate Mousse

1 cup (6 ounces) semi-sweet
   chocolate chips
1 (14-ounce) can EAGLE®
   Brand Sweetened
   Condensed Milk (NOT
   evaporated milk)

1½ teaspoons vanilla extract
2 cups (1 pint) BORDEN® or
   MEADOW GOLD®
   Whipping Cream, whipped
   (do not use non-dairy
   whipped topping)

In medium saucepan, melt chips; remove from heat. Add sweetened condensed milk and vanilla; mix well. Cool to room temperature or chill 20 to 30 minutes. Fold in whipped cream. Spoon equal portions into individual serving dishes. Freeze 2 hours or until firm. Garnish as desired. Freeze leftovers.   *Makes 6 to 8 servings*

Tropical Frozen Mousse

2½ cups mango chunks (2 to
    4 mangos, peeled and cut
    into bite-size pieces)
⅓ cup sugar
1 tablespoon kirsch

1 teaspoon fresh lime juice
¼ teaspoon grated lime peel
2 cups whipped cream
    Mango slices and fresh mint
    leaves for garnish

Place mango chunks in food processor or blender container. Cover; process until smooth. Blend in sugar, kirsch, lime juice and lime peel. Fold whipped cream into mango mixture. Pour into sherbet glasses or freezer tray. Cover and freeze 4 hours or until firm. Let stand at room temperature 30 minutes before serving. Garnish with mango slices and mint leaves just before serving.

Makes 6 servings

Peach Ice Cream Charlotte

1 package (3 ounces)
    ladyfingers, thawed if
    frozen and split in half
    horizontally
1 quart peach ice cream,
    softened
¼ cup chopped almonds, toasted
    (see Tip page 39)

3 tablespoons almond liqueur or
    2 teaspoons almond extract
1 cup whipping cream
1 tablespoon confectioners'
    sugar
¼ teaspoon almond extract
    Sliced almonds
    Sliced peaches

Butter bottom and side of charlotte mold or 2½-quart bowl. Line side and bottom with ladyfingers, cut side facing in; set aside. Combine peach ice cream, almonds and almond liqueur in medium bowl. Spoon into mold. Freeze several hours or overnight. Remove mold from freezer; dip in warm water. Unmold onto serving plate. Return to freezer up to 3 hours. Just before serving, combine whipping cream, sugar and extract in large bowl. Beat until stiff peaks form. Pipe through pastry tube fitted with fluted tip onto top of mold. Garnish with almonds and peaches. Serve immediately.

Makes 1 cake

Favorite recipe from **American Dairy Association**

Tropical Frozen Mousse

Peppermint Ice Cream Gems

Peppermint Ice Cream Gems

3 cups finely crushed creme-
   filled chocolate sandwich
   cookies (about 34 cookies)
½ cup margarine or butter,
   melted
1 (14-ounce) can EAGLE®
   Brand Sweetened
   Condensed Milk (NOT
   evaporated milk)
¼ cup white creme de menthe or
   ½ teaspoon peppermint
   extract

2 tablespoons peppermint
   schnapps
   Red or green food coloring,
   optional
2 cups (1 pint) BORDEN® or
   MEADOW GOLD®
   Whipping Cream, whipped
   (do not use non-dairy
   whipped topping)

Combine crumbs and margarine. Using back of spoon, press 2 rounded
tablespoons crumb mixture in bottom and up side of 24 (2½-inch)
paper-lined muffin cups. In large mixer bowl, combine sweetened
condensed milk, creme de menthe, schnapps and food coloring if
desired. Fold in whipped cream. Spoon mixture into prepared cups.
Freeze 6 hours or until firm. To serve, remove paper liners. Garnish as
desired. Freeze leftovers.   *Makes 2 dozen*

Frozen Piña Colada Torte

1 (7-ounce) package flaked
   coconut, toasted (2⅔ cups)
   (see Tip page 18)
3 tablespoons margarine or
   butter, melted
1 (14-ounce) can EAGLE®
   Brand Sweetened
   Condensed Milk (NOT
   evaporated milk)
½ cup COCO LOPEZ® Cream of
   Coconut

1 (20-ounce) can crushed
   pineapple, well drained
2 cups (1 pint) BORDEN® or
   MEADOW GOLD®
   Whipping Cream, whipped
   (do not use non-dairy
   whipped topping)
Maraschino cherries

Reserving ¾ cup coconut, combine remaining coconut and margarine; press firmly on bottom of 9-inch springform pan, 13×9-inch baking pan *or* 9-inch square pan. In large bowl, combine sweetened condensed milk and cream of coconut; stir in 1 cup pineapple. Fold in whipped cream. Pour half the mixture into prepared pan. Sprinkle with ½ cup reserved coconut; top with remaining cream mixture. Cover; freeze 6 hours or until firm. Just before serving, garnish with remaining coconut, remaining pineapple and cherries. Freeze leftovers.

Makes 12 to 15 servings

Pineapple Pistachio Dessert

1 can (8 ounces) DOLE®
   Crushed Pineapple in juice,
   drained
2 ounces chopped DOLE®
   Pistachios

2 tablespoons orange-flavored
   liqueur
Grated peel from 1 DOLE®
   Orange
1 quart vanilla ice cream,
   softened

Gently fold pineapple, pistachios, liqueur and orange peel into ice cream. Turn into 1½-quart mold. Freeze 4 hours or until firm. Dip bottom of mold in hot water for 20 seconds to unmold. Invert onto serving plate. Garnish as desired. *Makes 6 servings*

Frozen Fruit Salad

1 (3½-ounce) can flaked
coconut, lightly toasted
(1⅓ cups) (see Tip
page 18)
3 tablespoons margarine or
butter, melted
1 (17-ounce) can fruit cocktail,
well drained
1 (14-ounce) can EAGLE®
Brand Sweetened
Condensed Milk (NOT
evaporated milk)
1 cup CAMPFIRE® Miniature
Marshmallows

1 cup chopped pecans
1 (8-ounce) container
BORDEN® or MEADOW
GOLD® Sour Cream
¾ to 1 cup chopped maraschino
cherries
½ cup REALIME® Lime Juice
from Concentrate
1 (4-ounce) container frozen
non-dairy whipped topping,
thawed (1¾ cups)

Line 9×5-inch loaf pan with aluminum foil, extending foil above sides
of pan. Combine coconut and margarine; press firmly on bottom of
prepared pan. In large bowl, combine remaining ingredients except
whipped topping; mix well. Fold in whipped topping. Pour into
prepared pan. Freeze 6 hours or until firm. To serve, remove from pan;
peel off foil. Garnish as desired. Slice to serve. Freeze leftovers.

Makes 8 to 10 servings

Pineapple Baked Alaska

1 large DOLE® Fresh Pineapple
1 pint ice cream or sorbet, any
flavor

4 egg whites, room temperature
¼ teaspoon cream of tartar
½ cup sugar

Cut pineapple in half lengthwise through crown. Remove fruit, leaving
shells intact. Turn shells upside down to drain. Core and dice fruit.
Reserve 2 cups for Baked Alaska; refrigerate remainder for another use.

Spread ice cream in shells. Cover with plastic wrap; freeze 4 hours or
until frozen. Top with pineapple. Return to freezer.

Preheat oven to 450°F. Beat egg whites and cream of tartar until soft
peaks form. Gradually add sugar, beating until glossy and stiff peaks
form. Spread meringue over pineapple, sealing edges well. Make peaks
in meringue with back of spoon. Cover crowns with foil. Bake 4 to 5
minutes until meringue is lightly browned. Remove foil. Serve
immediately.

Makes 6 servings

Banana Split Square

Banana Split Squares

1 (21.5- or 23.6-ounce)
   package fudge brownie mix
2 bananas, thinly sliced, dipped
   in REALEMON® Lemon
   Juice from Concentrate and
   drained
½ cup chopped nuts, optional

2 quarts plus 1 pint BORDEN®
   or MEADOW GOLD® Ice
   Cream, any 3 flavors,
   softened
Chocolate ice cream topping,
   whipped cream, banana
   slices, nuts, cherries

Preheat oven to 350°F. Prepare brownie mix as package directs; spread in 13×9-inch baking pan. Bake 20 to 25 minutes; cool. On brownie, layer bananas, nuts, 1 quart ice cream, 1 pint ice cream and 1 quart ice cream. Cover; freeze 6 hours or until firm. Remove from freezer 10 minutes before serving. Cut into squares; garnish with ice cream topping, whipped cream, banana slices, nuts and cherries. Freeze leftovers. *Makes 12 to 16 servings*

Ice Cream Cookie Sandwich

2 pints chocolate chip ice
   cream, *softened*
1 package DUNCAN HINES®
   Moist Deluxe Dark Dutch
   Fudge Cake Mix

½ cup butter or margarine,
   softened

1. Line bottom of one 9-inch round cake pan with aluminum foil. Spread ice cream in pan. Return to freezer until firm. Run knife around edge of pan to loosen ice cream. Remove from pan. Wrap in foil and return to freezer.

2. Preheat oven to 350°F. Line bottom of two 9-inch round cake pans with aluminum foil. Place cake mix in large bowl. Add butter. Mix until crumbs form. Place half the cake mix in each pan. Press lightly. Bake at 350°F for 15 minutes or until browned around edges; do not overbake. Cool 10 minutes. Remove from pans. Remove foil from cookie layers. Cool completely.

3. To assemble, place cookie layer on serving plate. Top with ice cream. Peel off foil. Place second cookie layer on top. Wrap in foil and freeze 2 hours. To keep longer, store in airtight container.

Makes 10 to 12 servings

Tip: You can use lemon sherbet and Duncan Hines Moist Deluxe Lemon Supreme Cake Mix in place of chocolate chip ice cream and Moist Deluxe Dark Dutch Fudge Cake Mix.

Frozen Mint Chocolate Mousse

1 (14-ounce) can EAGLE®
   Brand Sweetened
   Condensed Milk
   (*NOT evaporated milk*)
⅔ cup chocolate flavored syrup
¾ teaspoon peppermint extract

1 cup (½ pint) BORDEN® or
   MEADOW GOLD®
   Whipping Cream, whipped
   (*do not use non-dairy
   whipped topping*)

In large bowl, combine sweetened condensed milk, syrup and extract; mix well. Fold in whipped cream. Spoon equal portions into individual serving dishes. Freeze 3 to 4 hours or until firm. Garnish as desired. Freeze leftovers.

Makes 6 to 8 servings

Truffle Treats

6 squares BAKER'S®
    Semi-Sweet Chocolate
¼ cup (½ stick) PARKAY®
    Margarine
2⅔ cups (7 ounces) BAKER'S®
    ANGEL FLAKE® Coconut
1 package (8 ounces)
    PHILADELPHIA BRAND®
    Cream Cheese, softened
2½ cups cold half and half or
    milk

1 package (6-serving size)
    JELL-O® Instant Pudding
    and Pie Filling, Chocolate
    Flavor
2 tablespoons unsweetened
    cocoa
1 tablespoon confectioners
    sugar

Place chocolate in heavy saucepan over very low heat; stir constantly until just melted. Remove 2 tablespoons of the melted chocolate; set aside.

Stir margarine into remaining chocolate in saucepan until melted. Gradually stir in coconut, tossing to coat evenly. Press mixture into 13×9-inch baking pan which has been lined with foil.

Beat cream cheese at medium speed of electric mixer until smooth; beat in reserved 2 tablespoons chocolate. Gradually mix in half and half. Add pudding mix. Beat at low speed until well blended, about 1 minute. Pour over crust. Freeze until firm, about 4 hours or overnight.

Mix together cocoa and sugar in small bowl; sift over truffle mixture. Lift with foil from pan onto cutting board; let stand 10 minutes to soften slightly. Cut into diamonds, squares or triangles.

Makes about 20 pieces

Prep time: 15 minutes
Freezing time: 4 hours

Acknowledgments

*The publishers would like to thank the companies and organizations
listed below for the use of their recipes in this publication.*

American Dairy Association
Blue Diamond Growers
Borden Kitchens, Borden, Inc.
Carnation, Nestlé Food Company
Checkerboard Kitchens, Ralston Purina Company
Cherry Marketing Institute, Inc.
Dole Food Company, Inc.
Dreyer's/Edy's Grand Ice Cream, Inc.
Florida Department of Citrus
Hershey Chocolate U.S.A.
Kahlúa Liqueur
Kraft General Foods, Inc.
Thomas J. Lipton Co.
Nabisco Foods Group
Nestlé Chocolate and Confection Company
Oklahoma Peanut Commission
Pollio Dairy Products
The Procter & Gamble Company, Inc.

Photo Credits

*The publishers would like to thank the companies and organizations
listed below for the use of their photographs in this publication.*

Blue Diamond Growers
Borden Kitchens, Borden, Inc.
Dole Food Company, Inc.
Hershey Chocolate U.S.A.
Kraft General Foods, Inc.
Nestlé Chocolate and Confection Company
The Procter & Gamble Company, Inc.

INDEX

continued